The New York Times

Guide to Making the New Tax Law Work for You

The New York Times

Guide to Making the New Tax Law Work for You

Karen W. Arenson

Times
BOOKS

Published by TIMES BOOKS, a division of
Quadrangle/The New York Times Book Co., Inc.
Three Park Avenue, New York, N.Y. 10016

Published simultaneously in Canada by
Fitzhenry & Whiteside, Ltd., Toronto

ISBN 0-8129-1010-9

Manufactured in the United States of America

ACKNOWLEDGMENTS

My thanks first to John M. Lee, business and financial news editor of The New York Times, whose idea it was to do a series on the new tax law, and who provided support and enthusiasm throughout the seven-week series. The many generous comments of others at The Times, including A. M. Rosenthal, executive editor, and Seymour Topping, managing editor, were helpful as well in the decision to expand the newspaper pieces into a full length book.

I also deeply appreciate the help I received from many accountants, lawyers and other tax experts, who spent long hours explaining the new law and its ramifications. Many of them were quoted in the series and are also quoted in this book.

As I worked on the book, some of these same people provided additional help by reading the manuscript. Herbert Paul of Touche Ross, Leon Nad of Price Waterhouse, and Peter Blank, editor of IRS Practice and Procedures, each read the book in near final form. Richard Reichler of Ernst & Whinney, David Rhine of Seidman & Seidman, Robert Castles of Arthur Young, and Matthew Maryles and Arthur Ainsberg of Oppenheimer & Company, all read individual chapters of the book.

Thanks also go to Leonard Schwartz of Times Books whose idea it was to do this book, to Patrick Filley, who edited the manuscript, and to Barth Healey, who did the final copyreading.

Finally, I am grateful to my friends and to my husband, Gregory Arenson, for their faith and encouragement.

Table of Contents

1
Why Cut Taxes

It may be hard to imagine that shaving $1,000 or $5,000 from your Federal tax bill could be good for the country, but that is the basic theory behind the new tax law, formally known as the Economic Recovery Tax Act of 1981. The message the White House sent to Congress in early 1981 was that burdensome taxes were strangling the economy. The result: massive tax cuts that could have the most revolutionary effect since the New Deal on your pocketbook, the nation's Treasury, and this country's economic well-being.

From a personal perspective, the immediate results of the new law seem clear. Not only will it lower personal income tax rates across the board, but it will also require significant changes in investment strategies and individual financial planning. Even family relationships could change. Such commonplace questions as, in whose name should the house or insurance policy be held, will require new answers because of the tax legislation of 1981.

For the average American, it will mean opportunities to avoid taxes on a certain amount of interest income and to set aside tax-free dollars for retirement. For the more well-to-do, the new law could affect the choice of tax shelters and other investments and how estates and gifts are to be arranged.

From a public policy perspective, however, the results of the new tax law are problematic. The sizable tax reductions could be just the solution needed by a stagnating economy. But, if the tax cuts backfire, they could send the economy into another round of spiralling inflation.

What brought about this dramatic change in tax policy was the rise in "supply-side economics." The supply-side economists, who are influential with Ronald Reagan, maintained that the trouble with the economy was not enough productivity. Increase productivity, they said, and inflation will go away and the economy will rebound.

Their argument was that because so much of everyone's earnings was taxed away, people were discouraged from working and from saving. After all, if the Government takes 50 cents or 70 cents out of every dollar you earn by working or by investing, how much incentive is there to work harder or invest more? Slash taxes, said the Reagan economists, and we will reverse these trends. We will spur people to work more and to save more. Their prescription: a sizable reduction in taxes, both for individuals and for business.

Many accepted the general theory that high taxes discouraged work and saving. But when it came to specifics, there was serious debate. How far did taxes have to fall to make people change their behavior? Would the tax cuts proposed by the administration be enough to make a difference? Everyone had different answers.

Talk of tax cuts also raised anew the specter of rampant inflation. While cutting taxes would be politically popular, cutting spending would be politically unpopular. But unless the Federal budget was reduced by at least the same amount as tax revenues, the country could face a larger deficit. The result, according to some critics, would be higher inflation.

For better or for worse, the Reagan administration got essentially what it asked for — and more. Personal tax rates were to be reduced by 23 percent, only slightly below the 27 percent the White House had sought. Corporate taxes were to be slashed nearly in half.

In the process, however, many other tax cuts were added as well, tax cuts that derisively came to be known as "Christmas tree baubles" and "fiscal grafitti": Reductions in the so-called windfall profits tax on oil revenues. Reductions in the taxes on estates and gifts. Reductions in the taxes on Americans working abroad. Reductions in the taxes on executive stock options. And so forth.

In fact, through the summer of 1981, Congressmen and Senators, Republicans and Democrats, began to compete with each other to see who could win the biggest tax cuts. Once it became clear that the cuts would pass, each Congressman looked for specific items that would help the constituents back home, and that would help him or her to win votes and financial backing. No one was surprised when Congressmen from states like Texas, Louisiana, and Oklahoma argued for lighter taxes on oil. Or when Congressmen from the industrial Northeast, including New York and Pennsylvania, backed bigger incentives for rehabilitating old buildings. Or when Congressmen from states with many resident high-technology companies, such as Massachusetts, proposed credits for research and development.

Of course, nothing was explained in terms of winning votes back home. Each new tax cut was presented as a means of helping the economy. The tax cuts for Americans working abroad, for example, was presented as a measure that would increase American exports. The logic? High taxes on Americans working abroad had made it too costly to send Americans to foreign countries. As a result, American multinational companies hired more and more foreigners to staff their offices overseas. These foreign employees, it was claimed, did not buy American equipment. When a German employee of an American company wanted to order automobiles, he ordered from Volkswagen. If the employee was Japanese, he ordered Toyotas. There simply were not enough Americans overseas ordering from General Motors or Ford. Or so the argument went. And the business lobbyists pressing for lower taxes on Americans abroad presented an economic study to support their contentions.

Perhaps the most controversial measure of all was the tax-exempt "All-Savers" certificates. By allowing a healthy chunk of the interest payments on a new category of saving certificate to be free of Federal tax, Congress hoped to help the ailing savings and loan industry to attract more money at lower interest rates. The problem with this strategy, as many observers were quick to point out, was that the cost to the Treasury would be an estimated $5 or $6 billion, and not all of the subsidy would be directed to the troubled thrift institutions. At least half of it was expected to go to commercial banks and other types of financial institutions that were also authorized to offer these certificates. One sponsor of the measure, expressing the dilemma he felt himself to be caught in, called it the worst bill he had ever introduced. But because of the political clout of the banks and savings associations, everyone was afraid to oppose it. It passed easily.

For a while, the administration tried to fight all of these midnight provisions. The White House goal had been a "clean bill": across-the-board tax cuts for individuals and for business, and nothing more. Anything else would simply put more pressure on the budget, jeopardizing the success of the administration's programs.

It soon became clear, however, that these extra measures were the price of getting the personal and business tax cuts through Congress. And a hefty price it was. The extra tax cuts added up to billions of dollars in additional tax savings for individuals and businesses — and billions of dollars in revenues lost to the Treasury.

Despite all the extras, on a foggy August 13, 1981, at his mountain ranch retreat in California, President Reagan signed into law what are potentially the most wide-reaching tax changes in this country's history. The impact of the new law, however, depends largely on how you respond to the opportunities presented.

The new law, for example, does not create new savings; it simply provides new incentives that could increase this country's savings rate. If you work, the new law lets you set up a tax-deferred savings account and put more money into it than ever before. It offers you the opportunity to shelter a certain amount of interest income from taxes, by investing in the tax-exempt savings certificates. If you put money into either type of account, you may be increasing the pool of savings — or you may not: If you take money from another savings account and move it into All-Savers plans, you will benefit from the tax savings, but you will not be adding to the country's pool of investment money. Only if you spend less and save more will the country's rate of savings increase.

The same is true of the work incentives in the new tax law. The Reagan administration hopes that by being allowed to keep more of the money you earn, you will work more productively and for longer hours. And, indeed, the lower tax rates may be an incentive to work, if you are not now employed, or to start a second business. If you do, you could benefit, and so could the country.

These incentives may also have the opposite effect. Some economists predict that lowering taxes may prompt people to work less: They contend that if you can earn the same amount of take-home pay by working fewer hours each week, you may opt for more leisure, rather than more income. If this happens, American productivity may fall, rather than rise.

The results will not become apparent for some time. It will take a while for people to understand what the new tax law offers and to decide which provisions, if any, they want to take advantage of. There are no simple answers, no iron-clad rules that say what will be best for everyone under the new law. Some provisions benefit some people, but not others. To take best advantage of the new tax law, you have to understand which measures suit you best.

This book does not try to dictate how you should respond to the law. It tries to explain what the opportunities are, and what you may gain or lose by pursuing them. It also tries to explain how to go make use of the provisions in the law that will work best for you. If you do nothing, the tax cuts alone could save you thousands of dollars. But with a little effort, the new tax law could save you even more than that. Perhaps, if we are lucky, it will bolster the economy as well.

2

An Overview
of the New Law

Taxes are a subject most of us would like to ignore. They reduce the money we can spend. The forms are complex, and filling them out can be a nightmare. It does not help that the new tax law is virtually unreadable.

With the passage of the law, however, grappling with your taxes is no longer something you can afford to relegate to a rainy afternoon in April. The law is chock-full of measures that can save you money. Some of the benefits are automatic, such as the cuts in individual income tax rates. But many of the potential benefits from the new law require action. You must buy the tax-exempt "All-Savers" certificates to be entitled to the tax exemption on the first $1,000 of interest income. You must set up an Individual Retirement Account to be eligible for tax-deferred savings and to enable you to reduce your taxable income. And you should be starting your planning now.

Even the benefits such as the income tax rate cuts, which require no effort on your part, could yield even bigger dividends with a little planning. For example, if you can delay any income, such as a bonus, until the next tax year, you will probably be in a lower tax bracket and could save some additional tax dollars. Similarly, you should speed up deductions where possible, since the deductions are worth more to you if you are in a higher tax bracket.

Don't be put off by the prospect of having to give some serious thought to your tax options. Under the new law, tax planning is no longer only for the rich: There is something in it for nearly everyone, provided you take advantage of what is available. No other tax law has offered so many different and varied opportunities.

In most cases, taking advantage of the tax-saving provisions in the new law may be a lot simpler than filling out your tax form. Setting up an Individual Retirement Account, for example, takes nothing more than opening a new bank or brokerage account. And by opening a special retirement account, you could reduce your taxes by as much as $1,000 in the first year alone.

The hard part is determining whether you are eligible, whether you have the money to invest, and how to invest it. What this book offers is a guide to answering many of these questions. What are the provisions in the new law? Who is eligible for the benefits? What do you have to do to take advantage of the opportunities that are there?

Knowing what is available will also give you a better idea of whether you need to consult an expert. In some cases, everything you need to do, you can do yourself. There are other areas, however, such as estate planning or tax shelters, where you should probably seek help from a lawyer, an accountant, or another specialist. If you do, it still makes sense to have an idea of what you can do under the new law. It will make your discussions with your financial adviser easier, and will increase your chances of accomplishing what you want.

Deductions, Credits, and Other Basic Tax Concepts

Before addressing the possibilities made available by the new law, it helps to understand such basic tax concepts as taxable income, deductions, and credits. These are the keys to the law. Most of the measures that can save you taxes, from the marriage penalty deduction to the child care credit, work by giving you either a deduction or a credit.

A deduction is an amount you are allowed to subtract from your income before calculating your tax. The tax code permits a wide array of deductions, including interest payments on a mortgage, charitable contributions, and business expenses. The new law may make it possible for you to claim larger deductions than ever. (Before calculating your tax, you are also allowed to subtact exemptions of $1,000 each, for yourself and each of your dependents, including your children. The new tax law does not change the $1,000 exemption until 1985, when it will be adjusted according to changes in consumer prices.)

Once you have figured out all of your deductions and exemptions, you will be able to calculate your taxable income, which is simply your total income after all the subtractions. It is this *taxable* income, not your *total* income, that determines your tax bracket. Your taxable income may be close to your total earnings. But it may also be a good deal less. For example, you could earn $35,000 and have taxable income of $30,000, or only $10,000. Although your total earnings would be the same in either case, the taxes you would pay would be very different. When you come across references to taxable income, do not automatically substitute your total earnings for that figure.

Once you have calculated your taxable income, you can look in the tax tables (Page 24) to find out how much tax you must pay and what your tax bracket is. When people refer to their tax brackets, they generally mean the percent of taxes they have to pay on their last dollar of earnings. If everybody paid the same rate of tax, say, 20 percent, your tax bracket would be the same as everyone else's. But the American tax system is progressive. That means that the more income you have, the higher the tax rate you generally pay.

The way the tax tables work, you pay gradually higher rates on each portion of your income. If you make $20,000, for example, you still pay the same rate of tax on your first $5,000 as someone who makes only $5,000. But your overall tax rate would be higher because your tax rates would be higher on the remaining $15,000. In this way, the last dollars you earn in any one year are taxed at a higher rate than the first dollars you earn.

If the highest rate you pay is 33 percent, you are in the 33 percent tax bracket. This figure is also called your marginal tax rate. This does not mean that you pay 33 percent of your income in tax. Nor do you pay 33 percent of your taxable income in tax. (If you calculated your taxes as a percent of your overall income, the percentage might be closer to 19 percent.) But the next dollar that you earn would be subject to a tax of 33 cents.

Even after you find your tax in the tax tables, you may be able to reduce this amount through tax credits. You may have credits for child care expenses, for certain business investments, or for foreign tax payments, to name a few possibilities. A dollar of tax credit is more valuable than a dollar of deduction. Each dollar of credit directly reduces your taxes by a dollar. Thus, $100 of tax credits are worth $100. That is considerably more than $100 of deductions would be worth. How much your deductions are worth depends on how much tax they save you, and that depends on your tax bracket. Their value is always smaller than the amount of the deduction.

A $100 deduction, for example, would permit you to subtract $100 from your income before your tax is calculated. If you were in the 50 percent tax bracket and had not been able to deduct $100, you would have had to pay $50 in taxes on the $100 of income. So in the 50 percent tax bracket, the $100 deduction would save you $50 in taxes. In the 30 percent bracket, a $100 deduction would save you only $30 in taxes. While the deduction is still attractive in the 30 percent bracket, it is clearly worth less than in the 50 percent bracket. In contrast, the tax credit is worth the same to everyone.

The Opportunities in the New Law

There are so many opportunities in the new tax law that it may be difficult to know where to begin. The new law could affect your plans for saving and investing, how many hours you decide to work — or whether you work at all, how much money you give to others, and how you structure your estate. It could open up jobs abroad, and it could influence whether you want your employer to reward you with stock options or some other incentive arrangement. All of these areas now warrant some rethinking.

Saving

Whether you are a confirmed saver, or whether you have never managed to keep more than $1,000 in the bank at any time, you should look into some of the incentives for saving under the new tax law. Basically, these incentives fall into two categories: the new, tax-exempt "All-Savers" certificates and the more generous provisions for tax-deferred retirement accounts. Since both work by allowing you to deduct certain amounts of money from your taxable income, the higher your tax bracket, the greater the benefit to you.

If you are in at least the 30 or 35 percent bracket, you should seriously consider investing in the certificates, which offer a kind of risk-free tax shelter. The certificates pay interest of up to 70 percent of the yield on one-year Treasury bills at the time of your purchase. Up to $1,000 of the income you earn on these certificates will be exempt from taxes no matter when you receive the interest, although the certificates will be sold for only a 15-month period, from October 1, 1981, to December 31, 1982. To take maximum advantage of the certificates, you would need to plan to invest about $8,000 or $9,000 for one year, depending on the interest rates at the time you made your investment.

There is nothing to bar you from buying the certificates if you are in a tax bracket below 30 percent. But you could probably do better investing in a money market fund or other investment vehicle: Although you would have to pay taxes on these other investments, your after-tax return might still be higher than your tax-free earnings from the certificates. Remember, exemption from tax should not be a goal in and of itself. It is only valuable if the amount you can earn on a tax-free basis is higher than what you can earn on other investments after you have paid tax.

Before you move all of your savings into savings certificates, you should also consider putting some money into a tax-deferred retirement plan. Virtually everyone who can afford to put money aside into such a plan ought to, although you will be limited to $2,000 a year. Any money you put into such a plan (generally known as an Individual Retirement

Account, or I.R.A.) is deductible from taxable income. Earnings on such an account are not currently taxable either. All of the money is taxed only when you withdraw it. But in the meantime, it has been able to accumulate interest free of taxes. There is a penalty for withdrawals made before you become 59½ years old.

Under the old tax law, you could not have an I.R.A. if you were covered by another pension plan. Beginning in 1982, you can. All you need is some kind of service income (wages or self-employment income, but not dividends or interest payments). "Everyone talks about tax shelters for the rich; this is a tax shelter for everyone," observes Herbert Paul, associate national tax director for Touche Ross. "I can't imagine a client I wouldn't advise to do this, even the very rich ones."

Self-employed persons and those with any kind of freelance income should also make use of the new tax law's more generous limits on contributions to Keogh plans, which take effect in 1982. The Keogh is simply another kind of tax-deferred pension plan. Depending on your income, you could place as much as $15,000 a year into a Keogh, deduct the deposit from your current taxable income, and allow it to accumulate interest tax-free until you withdraw the funds sometime after age 59½. You are limited to annual contributions of no more than 15 percent of your earned income.

Investing

If you are an investor, the new tax law is good reason to review your investment strategies, both with an eye to the benefits of the new tax code and from the perspective of how the economy might react to the new law. There could be shifts in the attractiveness of various companies and industries, as well as in the attractiveness of one type of investment versus another.

A new ceiling on the tax paid on long-term capital gains has already taken effect; you will now pay no more than 20 percent, down from the previous maximum of 28 percent. Some investment advisers think this could boost the stock market and other investments, such as venture capital, where a major portion of your investment return can come in the form of capital gains. They caution, however, that tax considerations alone should not determine your investments. Other factors, such as price and potential return, should be as important as ever.

Tax shelters are another investment area that is likely to change dramatically under the new law. For one thing, since the law slashes the top tax rate to 50 percent from 70, investors looking for big tax reductions through tax shelters may no longer be as interested in them. On the other hand, tax shelter sponsors are already restructuring their projects to appeal more to people in lower tax brackets, and to make other accommodations to the law. As a general rule, shelters that were attractive mostly for tax reasons are expected to look less inviting, while shelters that put more emphasis on economic return should look better than ever.

Working

The new tax law does not directly reward you for holding a job. But lower tax rates mean that you will be allowed to keep a greater portion of your earnings. The lower tax rates, combined with tax cuts for business, may also make this an opportune time to turn a hobby into a part-time business or to expand the small business you already run.

If you do not work, there are several measures in the new tax law that may make working more attractive economically. A married couple can not take advantage of the new marriage penalty deduction unless both spouses work. The same is true of the tax credits for child care expenses; if you pay for child care to enable you and your spouse to work, you could be eligible for a tax credit of hundreds of dollars. (This credit is also available to single persons who pay for child care to enable them to work.) The broader provisions for tax-deferred retirement accounts would also allow you to shelter the first $2,000 of your earned income from taxes. None of these provisions may matter as much as the type of job you could get or what you would be paid but, taken together, they may help to make working more attractive.

And if you've had a yen to work overseas, the new law could make such a position more attractive. It is also likely to open up new jobs abroad, since the lower taxes on expatriates will make it less costly for American corporations to maintain employees abroad.

Estates and Gifts

Perhaps the most dramatic change in the new tax law affects estates and gifts. Not only does the law permit you to give unlimited amounts to your spouse, tax-free, either while you are alive or after your death, but it significantly increases the amounts you can give tax-free to others as well. For all but a few, it will virtually abolish the estate tax. You may also want to change your plans for giving gifts while you are alive. The new law permits you to give tax-free gifts of $10,000 per recipient each year, beginning in 1982, more than triple the previous limit of $3,000.

That does not mean you can now skip estate and gift planning: You may need to make changes in your will. And if estate taxes are now less of a concern, that simply means you can concentrate more on other matters, such as the tax implications of your giving plans.

For example, under the new code, it would be more desirable for you to inherit your home from your spouse than to be the partial owner of the home at the time of your spouse's death. That is because any asset left to a spouse would be revalued — for tax purposes — at the time of death, based on its market price at that time rather than its original purchase price, which was probably lower. Thus, if you sell the house sometime after your spouse dies, the profit would be smaller for tax purposes, and so the tax on that profit would be less.

"People are going to have to go back and reconsider all of their holdings," says Peter Elinsky, a partner at the accounting firm of Peat, Marwick, Mitchell. "They shouldn't fall into the trap of thinking there is no tax impact on estates any more, so they can ignore it."

Other Changes

While the provisions above, aimed at the individual, have attracted the most attention, there are other measures, too, that could benefit you.

CHARITABLE CONTRIBUTIONS: Beginning in 1982, there will be a five-year period during which you will be allowed to take a deduction for charitable contributions, even if you do not itemize deductions. For 1982 and 1983, you will be allowed to deduct 25 percent of your first $100 of contributions, or a maximum of $25. In 1984, you will be allowed to deduct 25 percent of your first $300 of contributions, giving you a new limit of $75. In 1985, the rules change again, to allow you to deduct 50 percent of any contributions you make. Finally, in 1986, you may deduct 100 percent of your contributions. In 1987 and after, however, you may not take any deductions for charitable contributions unless you itemize all of your personal deductions, rather than taking a standard deduction.

SELLING A HOME: If you sell your home, you now have two years to buy another that costs at least as much as your old home in order to defer paying taxes on profits from the sale of your home. Under the old law, you had 18 months (unless you were building a new home, in which case you did have two years). The new rule applies to home sales made after July 20, 1981, as well as to homes sold no more than 18 months prior to that date.

Under the old tax law, you were allowed to exclude from taxes profits of up to $100,000 on the sale of your home, if you were 55 or older. The new law lifts that one-time exclusion to $125,000 for a house sold after July 20, 1981.

ADOPTION ASSISTANCE: The law now provides a deduction of up to $1,500 to help cover the expenses of adopting a hard-to-place child whom the government has decided can not be placed without adoption assistance. The government gives ongoing "maintenance" payments for such children, but had not, until now, provided any help with adoption fees, court costs, and attorney's fees involved with adoption. The new deduction is available only to those who itemize deductions.

The array of options could be somewhat overwhelming at first. But if you get a rough idea of which areas are most likely to apply to you, and then consider them one by one, the task should be manageable. These steps will not make your taxes disappear altogether. They will not make you a millionaire. They will not make filling out your tax form any easier. But they may make it less painful, by reducing your taxes. The possible savings are very real, for those who go after them.

3

The Personal Tax Cuts

On October 1, 1981, the much-heralded income tax cuts began, the cuts that were the original centerpiece of the Reagan economic program. The theory was simple: High tax rates deter people from working. Lower rates would encourage people to work harder, and thus boost the economy. As for the reality, that is a matter of some controversy among economists.

The new tax law mandated that tax rates on individual income be reduced by 5 percent on October 1, 1981; by 10 percent on July 1, 1982, and by another 10 percent on July 1, 1983. The total reduction will amount to a 23 percent cut in tax rates (and not 25 percent, because of the way the percentages are calculated).

You have probably already noticed some reduction in tax withheld from your paychecks. For most, it probably did not amount to more than $5 or $10 a week. While the second and third steps of the tax cut will be larger, tax specialists caution that you still should not expect big reductions. "We're not really cutting taxes for most people, we are simply preventing their taxes from going higher," says Leon M. Nad, a partner at the accounting firm of Price Waterhouse. While tax rates are being reduced, he notes, inflation will push most salaries higher. Thus, the tax cuts will simply offset the extra taxes you would have had to pay on higher wages. "If you continued to earn the same amount of taxable income, you would see a real saving," Mr. Nad says.

The law also sliced the maximum tax on individual income to 50 percent, effective January 1, 1982, from the current ceiling of 70 percent. (There is already a 50 percent ceiling on earned income such as wages, salaries, pensions, and bonuses, but not on unearned income such as interest payments, dividends, and rent.) "People in these brackets are really getting the biggest tax break," says James E. Power, a tax partner at Deloitte Haskins & Sells. Moving from a 70 percent tax bracket to a 50 percent tax bracket represents a cut of 29 percent.

Deloitte Haskins & Sells, the accounting firm, has calculated some typical reductions people will see, provided they have no increases in income over the period of the tax cuts:

In 1980, a married couple with taxable income of $25,000 would have been in the 32 percent tax bracket and would have paid $4,633 in taxes. In 1984, a couple with the same taxable income will be in the 25 percent tax bracket and pay $3,565, or $1,068 less.

In 1980, a couple with taxable income of $75,000 would have been in the 54 percent tax bracket and would have paid $27,778 in taxes. In 1984, that amount of taxable income will place the couple in the 42 percent tax bracket, with a tax bill of $21,468, or $6,310 less than in 1980.

When the tax cuts are complete, another kind of tax reduction program will be put in place. That program, known as indexing, will peg the tax system to the Consumer Price Index, beginning January 1, 1985. Each year, tax brackets, exemptions and the standard deduction will be raised by the same amount that prices have risen. Under this system, as your income rises, you will not be pushed into a higher tax bracket unless your income has risen by more than the rate of inflation.

Consider a simple example, in which your salary is $100 and your tax is $20, or 20 percent of your salary. If inflation is 10 percent, and you get a 10 percent raise, you have no more purchasing power than you did previously. You would be making $110, but everything you bought would cost 10 percent more. Under the old tax system, not only would you have had to pay more taxes, but you would have had to pay a

Tax Liabilities and Marginal Tax Rates*

The following tables illustrate how the tax burden will be decreased over the next 3 years for married couples filing joint returns and unmarried individuals. The marginal tax rate columns indicate the rate of tax at which the next dollar of income would be taxed in 1980 and in 1984.

Couples Filing Joint Returns

Taxable Income	1980	1981	Tax Liability 1982
$15,000	$2,055	$2,029	$1,823
$25,000	$4,633	$4,575	$4,153
$35,000	$8,088	$7,987	$7,257
$50,000	$14,778	$14,593	$13,305
$75,000	$27,778	$27,431	$25,055
$100,000	$41,998	$41,473	$37,449
$150,000	$73,528	$72,609	$62,449
$200,000	$107,032	$105,694	$87,449

Unmarried Individuals

Taxable Income	1980	1981	Tax Liability 1982
$15,000	$2,605	$2,572	$2,330
$25,000	$5,952	$5,878	$5,362
$35,000	$10,207	$10,079	$9,208
$50,000	$18,067	$17,841	$16,318
$75,000	$33,393	$32,976	$28,818
$100,000	$50,053	$49,427	$41,318
$150,000	$84,887	$83,826	$66,318
$200,000	$119,887	$118,388	$91,318

*Ordinary Rates—Without Regard to Special Rates for Capital Gains, Income Averaging, or Maximum Tax on Earned Income.

1983	1984	Reduction in Tax 1980-84	Marginal Tax Rate 1980	1984
$1,676	$1,581	$474	21%	16%
$3,760	$3,565	$1,068	32%	25%
$6,564	$6,218	$1,870	37%	28%
$12,014	$11,368	$3,410	49%	38%
$22,614	$21,468	$6,310	54%	42%
$34,190	$32,400	$9,598	59%	45%
$59,002	$56,524	$17,004	64%	49%
$84,002	$81,400	$25,632	68%	50%

1983	1984	Reduction in Tax 1980-84	Marginal Tax Rate 1980	1984
$2,097	$2,001	$604	30%	23%
$4,829	$4,565	$1,387	39%	30%
$8,313	$7,849	$2,358	49%	38%
$14,738	$13,889	$4,178	55%	42%
$26,973	$25,571	$7,822	63%	48%
$39,473	$37,935	$12,118	68%	50%
$64,473	$62,935	$21,952	70%	50%
$89,473	$87,935	$31,952	70%	50%

higher percentage of your income in taxes. After inflation, because you were pushed into a higher tax bracket, you might have had to pay 25 percent of your new salary, instead of 20 percent.

Under indexing, if you are paying 20 percent of your income in tax, you will continue to pay 20 percent if your salary rises by no more than the Consumer Price Index. Thus you will pay 20 percent of $110, or $22. But to the extent that your salary rises faster than inflation, you will have a real gain in purchasing power, but you may move to a higher tax bracket, where you will pay a somewhat higher rate of tax.

Until indexing begins in 1985, however, the tax cuts will perform roughly the same function as indexing. If inflation turns out to be less than the 23 percent tax cuts, people will actually see their taxes fall. If inflation exceeds the cuts, people will see their taxes rise.

Compared to most of the other provisions in the new tax law, the rate cuts are simple to apply. Everyone who pays income taxes qualifies for the rate cuts. This is one area of the new law that does not require individuals to do anything special to benefit. Employers are required to reduce their withholding taxes to conform to the new tax rates, but employees need not do anything.

But while the rate cuts are simple to use, they can be somewhat confusing to understand. For example, although the three tax cuts are set at 5 percent, 10 percent, and 10 percent, the total tax reduction will total 23 percent, not 25 percent. That is because the second and third reductions will be on tax rates that have already been reduced.

Thus, the first cut of 5 percent would reduce a hypothetical $100 tax bill to $95. The next cut would be 10 percent of $95, or $9.50, not 10 percent of the original $100 tax bill. That would reduce the tax bill to $85.50. The same shrinkage would occur in the third tax cut, 10 percent of $85.50, or $8.55. That would bring the tax bill down to $76.95, or, to be precise, 23.05 percent below its level before the tax cuts took effect.

Another complicating factor is that the cuts have not been timed to coincide with calendar years. Therefore, people should not look for their tax bills to fall neatly by 5 percent or 10 percent each year. If the first tax cut, of 5 percent, had occurred on January 1, 1981, rather than on October 1, people would have paid 5 percent less taxes for the whole year. But since the lower rate was not effective until the last quarter of the year, the 1981 tax will fall by 1.25 percent (one-quarter of 5 percent), rather than by 5 percent. By the end of 1982, tax rates will have fallen by 11 percent. By the end of 1983, they will have dropped 19 percent. And not until 1984 will the full 23 percent reduction in rates apply to the whole year.

While the first tax cut did not take effect until October 1, the rate reduction is to be applied to income earned any time during the year, not just to income earned after the tax cut goes into effect. The Government will apply a 1.25 percent cut to all income earned during the year, rather than applying a 5 percent tax cut to income earned only in the last three months of 1981.

"You would run into very practical problems trying to isolate most kinds of income into discrete periods during the year," says Mr. Nad, of Price Waterhouse. "You would also have to allocate deductions and exemptions over the year. That's why it is being handled this way."

If you have taxable income of less than $50,000, there will be no need to calculate your tax payments for 1981. The Internal Revenue Service prepares special tables showing your taxes for any given level of taxable income. These tables will take into account the 1.25 percent tax credit calculation. The figure in this special table should be close to what you would have arrived at had you calculated your own taxes from the basic tax tables and then subtracted a 1.25 percent credit.

If your income is $50,000 or more, you will have to look up your tax bracket and calculate your own taxes from the basic tax tables. You will calculate your taxes according to the old tax rates, and then reduce the total by a tax credit equal to 1.25 percent of the total due under the old schedules. This approach means that a person who worked only from January to March, before the tax cut went into effect, will be eligible for the same tax reduction as one who worked only from October to December, after the tax cut took effect.

Tax experts say that some quirks will arise under this method of calculation. For example, Congress mandated that the the maximum tax on long-term capital gains taken after June 9, 1981, would be 20 percent. But since the capital gains calculation takes place before the total tax bill is reduced by 1.25 percent, this brings the effective rate on capital gains down to a maximum of 19.75 percent in 1981. "There is some indication that Congress meant the maximum capital gains tax to be 20 percent and not 19.75 percent, so they could pass a technical correction before 1981 is out," Mr. Nad says.

Similarly, people subject to the 50 percent maximum tax on earned income in 1981 will actually be paying something less than 50 percent — 49.375 percent to be precise. After 1981, however, the tax tables will be revised, and there will no longer be a special credit of 1.25 percent, or of any other amount, to wreck havoc with the other tax rates. "There's a funny twist here," remarks Mr. Power of Deloitte Haskins & Sells. While everyone else will be paying lower tax rates in 1982 than in 1981, he says, "These people in the 50 percent tax bracket may actually see their taxes go up between 1981 and 1982 — to the full 50 percent, rather than 49.375 percent."

Q: First I heard that the 1981 tax cut would be 5 percent. Then I heard that it would be much smaller. Which is it?

A: If the first tax cut, of 5 percent, had occurred on January 1, 1981, rather than October 1, your taxes would have fallen by 5 percent. But since the tax cut was effective only for one quarter of the year, your taxes for the year will fall only by one quarter of 5 percent, or 1.25 percent.

Q: I worked for the first six months of 1981, but did not work the rest of the year. Will I be eligible for the 1981 tax cut?

A: Yes. While the tax cut did not become effective until October 1, the 1.25 percent tax reduction will apply to any income earned during the year, no matter when.

Q: I am retired and I no longer have a salary, only investment income. Will the income tax cuts apply to investment income as well as to salaries?

A: Yes. The personal income tax cut applies to all income earned by individuals. It does not apply to income earned by corporations, since there are separate tax cuts for corporations. The cuts in individual income tax rates would, for example, affect wages, salaries, self-employment income, and bonuses as well as interest, dividends, royalties, and capital gains.

Q: My friends say that indexing our tax system is bad. Is it?

A: Indexing will prevent you from being taxed at ever-higher rates during a period of inflation, unless Congress intentionally votes for higher tax rates. Although higher tax rates were a burden to individuals, they made it easier for the Government to finance its increasing costs.

Congress could still vote for higher taxes if they wish, but that is often seen as a politically unpopular position to take. So some people fear that indexing is likely to widen the Federal budget deficit, which to some people is an anathema. Other people, however, feel that the lower tax revenues will be a good incentive to cut back Government spending and to narrow the role of Government. To still others, this would be a negative.

One other problem, some critics contend, is that indexing insulates people from the problems of inflation, so they may not be as motivated to fight it. The response to this criticism is that without indexing, many people are hurt by inflation. And having the incentive does not necessarily mean that you will be able to conquer the problem.

Chart A
Joint Returns

If taxable income is:	The tax is:
Not over $3,400	No tax.
Over $3,400 but not over $5,500	14% of excess over $3,400.
Over $5,500 but not over $7,600	$294, plus 16% of excess over $5,500.
Over $7,600 but not over $11,900	$630, plus 18% of excess over $7,600.
Over $11,900 but not over $16,000	$1,404, plus 21% of excess over $11,900.
Over $16,000 but not over $20,200	$2,265, plus 24% of excess over $16,000.
Over $20,200 but not over $24,600	$3,273, plus 28% of excess over $20,200.
Over $24,600 but not over $29,900	$4,505, plus 32% of excess over $24,600.
Over $29,900 but not over $35,200	$6,201, plus 37% of excess over $24,600.
Over $35,200 but not over $45,800	$8,162, plus 43% of excess over $35,200.
Over $45,800 but not over $60,000	$12,720, plus 49% of excess over $45,800.
Over $60,000 but not over $85,600	$19,678, plus 54% of excess over $60,000.
Over $85,600 but not over $109,400	$33,502, plus 59% of excess over $85,600.
Over $109,400 but not over $162,400	$47,544, plus 64% of excess over $109,400.
Over $162,400 but not over $215,400	$81,464, plus 68% of excess over $162,400.
Over $215,400	$117,504, plus 70% of excess over $215,400.

* To calculate your taxes for 1981, use the 1980 tax and then subtract 1¼% (.0125) of the total.

1982	1983	1984 and after
The tax is:	**The tax is:**	**The tax is:**
No tax.	No tax.	No tax.
12% of the excess over $3,400.	11% of the excess over $3,400.	11% of the excess over $3,400.
$252, plus 14% of the excess over $5,500.	$231, plus 13% of the excess over $5,500.	$231, plus 12% of the excess over $5,500.
$546, plus 16% of the excess over $7,600.	$504, plus 15% of the excess over $7,600.	$483, plus 14% of the excess over $7,600.
$1,234, plus 19% of the excess over $11,900.	$1,149, plus 17% of the excess over $11,900.	$1,085, plus 16% of the excess over $11,900.
$2,012, plus 22% of the excess over $16,000.	$1,846, plus 19% of the excess over $16,000.	$1,741, plus 18% of the excess over $16,000.
$2,937, plus 25% of the excess over $20,200.	$2,644, plus 23% of the excess over $20,200.	$2,497, plus 22% of the excess over $20,200.
$4,037, plus 29% of the excess over $24,600.	$3,656, plus 26% of the excess over $24,600.	$3,465, plus 25% of the excess over $24,600.
$5,574, plus 33% of the excess over $29,900.	$5,034, plus 30% of the excess over $29,900.	$4,790, plus 28% of the excess over $29,900.
$7,323, plus 39% of the excess over $35,200.	$6,624, plus 35% of the excess over $35,200.	$6,274, plus 33% of the excess over $35,200.
$11,457, plus 44% of the excess over $45,800.	$10,334, plus 40% of the excess over $45,800.	$9,772, plus 38% of the excess over $45,800.
$17,705, plus 49% of the excess over $60,000.	$16,014, plus 44% of the excess over $60,000.	$15,168, plus 42% of the excess over $60,000.
$30,249, plus 50% of the excess over $85,600.	$27,278, plus 48% of the excess over $85,600.	$25,920, plus 45% of the excess over $85,600.
$30,249, plus 50% of the excess over $85,600.	$38,702, plus 50% of the excess over $109,400.	$36,630, plus 49% of the excess over $109,400.
$30,249, plus 50% of the excess over $85,600.	$38,702, plus 50% of the excess over $109,400.	$62,600, plus 50% of the excess over $162,400.
$30,249, plus 50% of the excess over $85,600.	$38,702, plus 50% of the excess over $109,400.	$62,600, plus 50% of the excess over $162,400.

Chart B
Heads of Households

If taxable income is:	The tax is:
Not over $2,300.	No tax.
Over $2,300 but not over $4,400	14% of excess over $2,300.
Over $4,400 but not over $6,500	$294, plus 16% of excess over $4,400.
Over $6,500 but not over $8,700	$630, plus 18% of excess over $6,500.
Over $8,700 but not over $11,800	$1,026, plus 22% of excess over $8,700.
Over $11,800 but not over $15,000	$1,708, plus 24% of excess over $11,800.
Over $15,000 but not over $18,200	$2,476, plus 26% of excess over $15,000.
Over $18,200 but not over $23,500	$3,308, plus 31% of excess over $18,200.
Over $23,500 but not ober $28,800	$4,951, plus 36% of excess over $23,500
Over $28,800 but not over $34,100	$6,859, plus 42% of excess over $28,800.
Over $34,100 but not over $44,700	$9,085, plus 46% of excess over $34,100.
Over $44,700 but not over $60,600	$13,961, plus 54% of excess over $44,700.
Over $60,600 but not over $81,800	$22,547, plus 59% of excess over $60,600.
Over $81,800 but not over $108,300	$35,055, plus 63% of excess over $81,800.
Over $108,300 but not over $161,300	$51,750, plus 68% of excess over $108,300.
Over $161,300.	$87,790, plus 70% of excess over $161,300.

* To calculate your taxes for 1981, use the 1980 tax and then subtract 1¼% (.0125) of the total.

1982	1983	1984 and after
The tax is:	**The tax is:**	**The tax is:**
No tax.	No tax.	No tax.
12% of the excess over $2,300	11% of the excess over $2,300	11% of the excess over $2,300
$252, plus 14% of the excess over $4,400.	$231, plus 13% of the excess over $4,400.	$231, plus 12% of the excess over $4,400.
$546, plus 16% of the excess over $6,500.	$504, plus 15% of the excess over $6,500.	$483, plus 14% of the excess over $6,500.
$898, plus 20% of the excess over $8,700.	$834, plus 18% of the excess over $8,700.	$791, plus 17% of the excess over $8,700.
$1,518, plus 22% of the excess over $11,800.	$1,392, plus 19% of the excess over $11,800.	$1,318, plus 18% of the excess over $11,800.
$2,222, plus 23% of the excess over $15,000.	$2,000, plus 21% of the excess over $15,000.	$1,894, plus 20% of the excess over $15,000.
$2,958, plus 28% of the excess over $18,200.	$2,672, plus 25% of the excess over $18,200.	$2,534, plus 24% of the excess over $18,200.
$4,442, plus 32% of the excess over $23,500.	$3,997, plus 29% of the excess over $23,500.	$3,806, plus 28% of the excess over $23,500.
$6,138, plus 38% of the excess over $28,800.	$5,534, plus 34% of the excess over $28,800.	$5,290, plus 32% of the excess over $28,800.
$8,152, plus 41% of the excess over $34,100.	$7,336, plus 37% of the excess over $34,100.	$6,986, plus 35% of the excess over $34,100.
$12,498, plus 49% of the excess over $44,700.	$11,258, plus 44% of the excess over $44,700.	$10,696, plus 42% of the excess over $44,700.
$20,289, plus 50% of the excess over $60,600.	$18,254, plus 48% of the excess over $60,600.	$17,374, plus 45% of the excess over $60,600.
$20,289, plus 50% of the excess over $60,600.	$28,430, plus 50% of the excess over $81,800.	$26,914, plus 48% of the excess over $81,800.
$20,289, plus 50% of the excess over $60,600.	$28,430, plus 50% of the excess over $81,800.	$39,634, plus 50% of the excess over $108,300.
$20,289, plus 50% of the excess over $60,600.	$28,430, plus 50% of the excess over $81,800.	$39,634, plus 50% of the excess over $108,300.

Chart C
Unmarried Individuals

1980

If taxable income is:	The tax is:
Not over $2,300.	No tax.
Over $2,300 but not over $3,400	14% of excess over $2,300.
Over $3,400 but not over $4,400	$154, plus 16% of excess over $3,400.
Over $4,400 but not over $6,500	$314, plus 18% of excess over $4,400.
Over $6,500 but not over $8,500	$692, plus 19% of excess over $6,500.
Over $8,500 but not over $10,800	$1,072, plus 21% of excess over $8,500.
Over $10,800 but not over $12,900	$1,555, plus 24% of excess over $10,800.
Over $12,900 but not over $15,000	$2,059, plus 26% of excess over $12,900.
Over $15,000 but not over $18,200	$2,605, plus 30% of excess over $15,000.
Over $18,200 but not over $23,500	$3,565, plus 34% of excess over $18,200.
Over $23,500 but not over $28,800	$5,367, plus 39% of excess over $23,500.
Over $28,800 but not over $34,100	$7,434, plus 44% of excess over $28,800.
Over $34,100 but not over $41,500	$9,766, plus 49% of excess over $34,100.
Over $41,500 but not over $55,300	$13,392, plus 55% of excess over $41,500.
Over $55,300 but not over $81,800	$20,982, plus 63% of excess over $55,300.
Over $81,800 but not over $108,300	$37,677, plus 68% of excess over $81,800.
Over $108,300.	$55,697, plus 70% of excess over $108,300.

* To calculate your taxes for 1981, use the 1980 tax and then subtract 1¼ % (.0125) of the total.

1982	1983	1984 and after
The tax is:	**The tax is:**	**The tax is:**
No tax.	No tax.	No tax.
12% of the excess over $2,300	11% of the excess over $2,300	11% of the excess over $2,300
$132, plus 14% of the excess over $3,400.	$121, plus 13% of the excess over $3,400.	$121, plus 12% of the excess over $3,400.
$272, plus 16% of the excess over $4,400.	$251, plus 15% of the excess over $4,400.	$241, plus 14% of the excess over $4,400.
$608, plus 17% of the excess over $6,500.	$251, plus 15% of the excess over $4,400.	$535, plus 15% of the excess over $6,500.
$948, plus 19% of the excess over $8,500.	$866, plus 17% of the excess over $8,500.	$835, plus 16% of the excess over $8,500.
$1,385, plus 22% of the excess over $10,800.	$1,257, plus 19% of the excess over $10,800.	$1,203, plus 18% of the excess over $10,800.
$1,847, plus 23% of the excess over $12,900.	$1,656, plus 21% of the excess over $12,900.	$1,581, plus 20% of the excess over $12,900.
$2,330, plus 27% of the excess over $15,000.	$2,097, plus 24% of the excess over $15,000.	$2,001, plus 23% of the excess over $15,000.
$3,194, plus 31% of the excess over $18,200.	$2,865, plus 28% of the excess over $18,200.	$2,737, plus 26% of the excess over $18,200.
$4,837, plus 35% of the excess over $23,500.	$4,349, plus 32% of the excess over $23,500.	$4,115, plus 30% of the excess over $23,500.
$6,692, plus 40% of the excess over $28,800.	$6,045, plus 36% of the excess over $28,800.	$5,705, plus 34% of the excess over $28,800.
$8,812, plus 44% of the excess over $34,100.	$7,953, plus 40% of the excess over $34,100.	$7,507, plus 38% of the excess over $34,100.
$12,068, plus 50% of the excess over $41,500.	$10,913, plus 45% of the excess over $41,500.	$10,319, plus 42% of the excess over $41,500.
$12,068, plus 50% of the excess over $41,500.	$17,123, plus 50% of the excess over $55,300.	$16,115, plus 48% of the excess over $55,300.
$12,068, plus 50% of the excess over $41,500.	$17,123, plus 50% of the excess over $55,300.	$28,835, plus 50% of the excess over $81,800.
$12,068, plus 50% of the excess over $41,500.	$17,123, plus 50% of the excess over $55,300.	$28,835, plus 50% of the excess over $81,800.

Chart D
Married Individuals Filing Separate Returns
1980

If taxable income is:	The tax is:
Not over $1,700.	No tax.
Over $1,700 but not over $2,750	14% of excess over $1,700.
Over $2,750 but not over $3,800	$147, plus 16% of excess over $2,750.
Over $3,800 but not over $5,950	$315, plus 18% of excess over $3,800.
Over $5,950 but not over $8,000	$702, plus 20% of excess over $5,950.
Over $8,000 but not over $10,100	$1,132.50, plus 24% of excess over $8,000.
Over $10,100 but not over $12,300	$1,636.50, plus 28% of excess over $10,100.
Over $12,300 but not over $14,950	$2,252.50, plus 32% of excess over $12,300.
Over $14,950 but not over $17,600	$3,100.50, plus 37% of excess over $14,950.
Over $17,600 but not over $22,900	$4,081, plus 43% of excess over $17,600.
Over $22,900 but not over $30,000	$6,360, plus 49% of excess over $22,900.
Over $30,000 but not over $42,800	$9,839, plus 54% of excess over $30,000.
Over $42,800 but not over $54,700	$16,751, plus 59% of excess over $42,800.
Over $54,700 but not over $81,200	$23,772, plus 64% of excess over $54,700.
Over $81,200 but not over $107,700	$40,732, plus 68% of excess over $81,200.
Over $107,700.	$58,752, plus 70% of excess over 107,700.

* To calculate your taxes for 1981, use the 1980 tax and then subtract 1¼% (.0125) of the total.

1982	1983	1984 and after
The tax is:	**The tax is:**	**The tax is:**
No tax.	No tax.	No tax.
12% of the excess over $1,700	11% of the excess over $1,700	11% of the excess over $1,700
$126, plus 14% of the excess over $2,750.	$115, plus 13% of the excess over $2,750.	$115, plus 12% of the excess over $2,750.
$273, plus 16% of the excess over $3,800.	$252, plus 15% of the excess over $3,800.	$241, plus 14% of the excess over $3,800.
$617, plus 19% of the excess over $5,950.	$574, plus 17% of the excess over $5,950.	$542, plus 16% of the excess over $5,950.
$1,006, plus 22% of the excess over $8,000.	$923, plus 19% of the excess over $8,000.	$870, plus 18% of the excess over $8,000.
$1,468, plus 25% of the excess over $10,100.	$1,322, plus 23% of the excess over $10,100.	$1,248, plus 22% of the excess over $10,100.
$2,018, plus 29% of the excess over $12,300.	$1,828, plus 26% of the excess over $12,300.	$1,732, plus 25% of the excess over $12,300.
$2,787, plus 33% of the excess over $14,950.	$2,517, plus 30% of the excess over $14,950.	$2,395, plus 28% of the excess over $14,950.
$3,661, plus 39% of the excess over $17,600.	$3,312, plus 35% of the excess over $17,600.	$3,137, plus 33% of the excess over $17,600.
$5,728, plus 44% of the excess over $22,900.	$5,167, plus 40% of the excess over $22,900.	$4,886, plus 38% of the excess over $22,900.
$8,852, plus 49% of the excess over $30,000.	$8,007, plus 44% of the excess over $30,000.	$7,584, plus 42% of the excess over $30,000.
$15,124, plus 50% of the excess over $42,800.	$13,639, plus 48% of the excess over $42,800.	$12,960, plus 45% of the excess over $42,800.
$15,124, plus 50% of the excess over $42,800.	$19,351, plus 50% of the excess over $54,700.	$18,315, plus 49% of the excess over $54,700.
$15,124, plus 50% of the excess over $42,800.	$19,351, plus 50% of the excess over $54,700.	$31,300, plus 50% of the excess over $81,200.
$15,124, plus 50% of the excess over $42,800.	$19,351, plus 50% of the excess over $54,700.	$31,300, plus 50% of the excess over $81,200.

4

The "All-Savers" Tax-Exempt Savings Certificate

No part of the new tax law has attracted so much attention as the tax-exempt savings certificates, also known as the "All-Savers" certificates. These certificates are basically one-year deposits at banks and other savings institutions, but they will be offered only between October 1, 1981, and December 31, 1982. What sets them apart from other certificates of deposit is that you as an individual may exempt up to $1,000 of interest earned from these certificates from Federal taxes. For a married couple filing a joint tax return, the exemption would be $2,000. Even before the new certificates became available on October 1, 1981, banks and thrift institutions were advertising them heavily, offering premiums and other inducements to sell their certificates.

From the start, the certificates were controversial. Their tax-exemption was expected to cost the Treasury more than $5 billion in forgone revenues. At the same time, no one was sure how much the certificates would help the beleaguered thrift industry or whether they would boost the savings rate, the two benefits suggested by the bankers promoting the idea. Nevertheless, because of the bankers' political clout, most Congressmen felt they had to vote for the certificates.

For many Americans, the certificates should be a boon. You probably should not be buying them if you are in a tax bracket of less than about 30 percent, since you can probably do better in other investments. But for others, the tax-free interest and the accessibility of the certificates should make them attractive. "Not only do the certificates provide tax-exempt income at a competitive rate, but they provide it in a risk-free form, because bank deposits are Government-insured," observes Susan G. Fisher, vice president and director of marketing for the Metropolitan division at Chemical Bank. "But," says Brian Glenn, a tax consultant at Coopers & Lybrand, "to be eligible for the tax exemption you have to tie up money for a whole year, and not everyone may be ready to do that."

How They Work

The new tax law sets the following rules:

WHO OFFERS THE CERTIFICATES: They may be offered by commercial and savings banks, savings and loan associations, credit unions, and other savings or thrift institutions supervised under Federal or state law. They may not be offered by money market funds.

WHEN: They may be offered at any time from October 1, 1981, to December 31, 1982, but each certificate would have only a one-year life.

HOW MUCH: Certificates must be available in denominations of $500, but may be offered in other denominations.

EARNINGS: Interest payments on the certificates will be set at 70 percent of the yield on new one-year Treasury bills at their most recent monthly auction. This means that the returns on the certificates will vary, depending on when you buy them. You should study interest rate forecasts before deciding when to buy. Once you purchase a certificate, its interest rate will not change during its one-year life.

The real attraction for most Americans is expected to be the tax-exemption. Each individual will be allowed to exclude up to $1,000 of interest earned on the All-Savers certificates from Federal tax. Couples filing joint tax returns will be able to exclude $2,000. Interest earned on other bank certificates of deposit will not be eligible for the exemption.

Who Should Buy the Certificates

Because the advantage of the certificates is their tax-exemption, they make better financial sense for some people than others. As a general rule, if you are in the 30 percent tax bracket or above, you probably should give serious consideration to the certificates. But if you are below the 30 percent tax bracket, you will probably do better putting your money into other investments, even though they are not tax-exempt. Tax-exemption is usually more valuable to those in the higher tax brackets. Of course, people above the 30 percent tax bracket may also find they can earn a higher after-tax return in other investments, but those investments are likely to carry more risk than the certificates.

You can see whether the certificates make sense for you by doing some calculations. First, look at how much you can earn, after tax, on other investments. Then compare that to how much you can earn on the savings certificates.

Let's say you can put your money in a one-year taxable investment paying 15 percent. This means you can earn $1,500 before tax on a $10,000 investment. If you are in a 50 percent Federal tax bracket, you keep only $750 after tax. In a 30 percent bracket, you would keep $1,050. And in a 10 percent bracket, the amount retained would grow to $1,350.

If the yield on the new tax-exempt savings certificates is 10.5 percent, a $10,000 investment would return $1,050, both before and after tax. That is clearly a better return than can be earned by people in tax brackets higher than 30 percent. But it is less than the after-tax rate available to people in tax brackets lower than 30 percent.

You should also include in your calculations taxes paid at the state and local levels. The certificates will be exempt from taxes in some states, but not in others, depending on each state's law. Many states automatically follow the Federal definition of income in deciding what to tax and what not to tax, unless they designate specific differences. These states are the ones most likely not to tax income from the certificates. But each state legislature has the option of changing that. Under the laws in effect when the certificates first became available, for example, the certificates would be exempt from taxes in New York and Connecticut, but not in New Jersey. Your local bank should be able to tell you about the rules in your state, or call your state tax office and ask.

How Much to Invest

If you decide that the savings certificates make sense for you, the next step is to figure out how much money you are going to need to invest to take full advantage of the maximum tax-exemption. Very roughly, to earn $1,000 in interest, each person should probably count on putting about $8,000 into the certificates, providing interest rates remain in the same range they were when the certificates became available on October 1, 1981. That $1,000 is the most an individual can exclude from taxes. (A couple, therefore, could not take maximum advantage of the tax exemption without putting about $16,000 into the certificates.)

The exact amounts will depend on the interest rate on the certificates at the time they are purchased. The amount of the certificate deposit needed could be less than $8,000, if interest rates soar. Or it could be more than $8,000, if rates fall. Let's say the certificates pay 12.5 percent. Then you would only have to put up $8,000 to earn $1,000 in interest. If you put $10,000 into certificates paying 12.5 percent, you would earn $1,250, but only $1,000 of that would be exempt from taxes. You would have to pay taxes on the remaining $250.

The next question is where you are going to take the money from. It could come out of other investments, such as stocks and bonds. It could come from another bank account or a money market fund. Or you may decide to take it out of your salary month by month.

In fact, there are many different strategies to consider in buying the certificates. Putting $8,000 in all at once may be more convenient, but it may not necessarily be the best policy. So if you do not have $8,000 to lock away all at once for a year, you shouldn't write off the certificates.

One alternative might be to put $4,000 into the certificates sometime in 1981. When they matured in 1982, the same money could be used to buy another $4,000 in certificates for another year. (Remember, the certificates will be available until December 31, 1982, but not after that.)

Or, you could try another strategy. If you don't think you'll have even $4,000 available to invest all at once, you might consider buying smaller amounts of certificates several times during the year. You might buy $500 of certificates or $1,000 of certificates each month. You could probably accumulate $1,000 in tax-exempt interest through any of these strategies.

Once you have managed to buy enough certificates to produce $1,000 in interest, stop. You've reached the limit of your tax-exemption. And it probably makes sense to look to other kinds of investments. The $1,000 tax exemption is not

---

This chart shows the amount you would have to invest in tax-exempt saving certificates to earn $1,000 in interest, the maximum each person can exempt from Federal taxes.

If the rate on 1-year Treasury bills is:	. . . then the rate on tax-exempt savings certificates will be:	To earn $1,000, you would have to invest this much in the tax-exempt saving certificates
12%	8.4%	$11,905
13%	9.19%	$10,989
14%	9.8%	$10,204
15%	10.5%	$9,524
16%	11.2%	$8,929
17%	11.9%	$8,403
18%	12.6%	$7,937
19%	13.3%	$7,519
20%	14.0%	$7,143

an exemption that is available each year. It is a one-time exemption for each person — though you can split it between two years, 1982 and 1983.

Despite the $1,000 cap on the tax exemption for an individual, there is no limit on how many certificates anyone can buy. But most people probably would not want to, since once the $1,000 tax-exemption has been used up, higher after-tax rates are available on other forms of investment.

For those people to whom the convenience and security of a bank is more attractive than the higher returns on other investments, the new tax-exempt certificates will offer a higher rate of interest than other one-year savings accounts now available.

Perhaps the biggest challenge to investors will be figuring out how best to buy the certificates, and whether to buy them all at once or spaced out during the 15 months they will be available. That will depend largely on your expectations of interest rates. If you think rates will rise, you should probably postpone your purchase. But if, in December 1982, you think there will be a large rise in rates, you may be better off not locking up your funds for a year, even to achieve the tax exemption. Tax experts caution that tax savings should be only part of the calculation, not the whole answer.

If you buy the certificates all at once, tax specialists suggest that you might want to buy them in small denominations, rather than in one large certificate — if there is a choice of denominations. By buying them in smaller denominations, you have more flexibility if you need to withdraw your money before the certificates mature in one year.

Of course, if you are fairly certain that you will need to reach some or all of your funds before the year is up, you will be better off investing in something other than the certificates, since there will be penalties for certificates redeemed early. Not only will you lose the tax exemption, but you will be required to forfeit — or pay — the equivalent of three months of interest as well. The tax law does not bar you from withdrawing your interest payments before the certificates mature. But if you do this, it would reduce the return on your certificate, which is calculated on the assumption that the interest compounds for a year, in other words, that you earn interest on the interest left in the account. Another caution: You should not plan to borrow to buy the certificates. If you do, the interest you pay on the money borrowed to purchase the certificates, unlike many other interest payments, may not be deducted from your taxable income.

How the Certificates Stack Up Against Other Taxable Investments Depending on Your Tax Bracket

	$8,000 invested in a taxable 1-year investment at 18 percent*		$8,000 invested in a tax-exempt savings certificate at 12.6 percent**	
TAX BRACKET (in pct.)	**RETURN**		**RETURN**	
	Before tax	After tax	Before tax	After tax
50%	$1,440	$720	$1,008	$1,004
40%	$1,440	$864	$1,008	$1,005
30%	$1,440	$1,008	$1,008	$1,006
20%	$1,440	$1,152	$1,008	$1,006
10%	$1,440	$1,296	$1,008	$1,007

* The yield on new one-year Treasury bills at their most recent auction prior to Oct. 1, 1981, the day tax-exempt certificates were first offered. Every month there is a new auction of one-year bills which determines the rate for the certificates for the following month.

** The yield on one-year tax-exempt savings certificates on Oct. 1, 1981, the day they were first offered. The yield changes every month after a new one-year Treasury bill auction is held, and is set at 70 percent of the yield on the new one-year bills.

After the Tax-Exempt Certificate

When you have used up your one-time $1,000 tax exemption, you will be finished with the tax-exempt certificate program. Congress could renew it, but most Congressional observers think that unlikely. In fact, to forestall the renewal of the program, Congress created a new program, to take effect in 1985, that would allow you to shelter some portion of your interest income from taxes.

Under the new plan, you would be allowed to deduct up to 15 percent of your interest earnings from your taxable income, up to a ceiling of a $450 deduction ($900 for married couples filing jointly). You would reach that limit if you earned $3,000 in interest income, since 15 percent of $3,000 is $450. Before you could calculate the exclusion, however, you would be required to subtract from your interest income any interest you pays on loans, except for mortgages and business loans. There has also been some discussion in Congress of raising those limits, but it would take another law to do that.

For the immediate future, you basically have two opportunities to earn income free from Federal tax. One is the tax-exempt savings certificates. The other is through tax-exempt retirement accounts, which are not really a means of avoiding tax so much as a way to defer it.

Perhaps the biggest difference between the two vehicles is in the time your money must remain invested. With the retirement account, you must be prepared for your savings to remain locked up until you reach age 59½. There are significant penalties if you withdraw funds earlier from the retirement account. (See Chapter 6.) The savings certificates, on the other hand, have a one-year maturity. While even that may be too long for some people, others should find the term quite reasonable. And do not be deterred from making some use of the tax-exemption programs even if you can not spare the full amounts allowed. They are not all-or-nothing plans. As Ben Franklin might have said today, "A penny of tax-savings is a penny earned."

Q: How do I buy a tax-exempt savings certificate?

A: You can buy them at any bank, savings bank, savings and loan association, credit union, or other Government-regulated savings institution. It's like opening a new bank account. The difference is that when it comes time to file your tax return, the interest you earn from these certificates — up to a limit of $1,000 for an individual — will not be subject to Federal tax.

Q: Will some banks offer higher rates on their certificates than others?

A: No. The law dictates the rate on the certificates: 70 percent of the yield on new one-year Treasury bills at their most recent auction. Your job will be to make the best decision you can about when rates will be highest, and to buy your certificates then.

Q: When is the best time to buy a tax-exempt certificate?

A: Choosing a time to buy a certificate will depend on two things. One is the availability of funds. There may be certain times of year, such as Christmas or when you file your tax return, when you have the least free cash available. There may be other times when you have more, such as if you get a bonus from your employer. In fact, if you don't have $8,000 to spend on certificates, don't. There is no requirement that you buy as much as $8,000. You could stop at $500, or $1,000, or $5,000.

The other factor is to try to invest when interest rates are highest. Trying to pick a peak in interest rates is tough. You can follow what is happening to the economy, and what economists and business executives are predicting. But even the professionals are often wrong. You should make your best guess, and pick a time when you will be satisfied with the rate, even if it turns out not to be the absolute highest you could have chosen. Because of the penalties for early withdrawal, however, be prepared to leave the money invested for the full year.

One other alternative is to spread your certificate purchases over the 15 months the certificates are available. There is no requirement that you have to buy $1,000 of certificates or $8,000 of certificates all at once. You could buy $1,000 a month for 8 months, or any other combination. While you would not necessarily get the highest interest rate during the year, you would get some kind of average of the rates available. Remember, the total amount of your purchases should be conditioned on interest rates and how much you will earn on your certificates. Your goal should be $1,000 of interest earnings, reached in any way you want.

Q: I already have some certificates of deposit at a bank. Will the interest on those be tax-exempt?

A: No. Only income from the specially designated certificates will be exempt from Federal taxes.

Q: Can I get a certificate through my money market fund?
A: No.

Q: I am in a tax bracket below 30 percent, but everybody says you should not buy these certificates unless you are above the 30 percent bracket. I want some tax-exempt income too. What should I do?

A: You would be allowed to buy the certificates, and the income would be exempt from taxes. But you can do better with other investments, even though you have to pay taxes on them. The fact of the matter is that tax exemption just for the sake of tax exemption isn't worth anything. Generally, tax-exempt investments provide more of an advantage the higher your tax bracket. Your goal should be to achieve the highest return after tax. If that is achieved through tax-exempt investments, fine. If it is achieved through taxable investments, that's OK, too. This is where you've got to take out your paper and pencil — or your pocket calculator — and figure out what's going to leave you with the most income after tax.

Q: I am single, with taxable income of about $20,000, and I am supposedly in a tax bracket over 30 percent. But my tax was just under $4,000, which is only 19 percent of my income. So I can't tell whether I should assume that I'm in the 30 percent-plus tax bracket and should buy the certificates, or whether I'm not really in the 30 percent bracket, and therefore probably should not buy them.

A: First, though you don't pay 30 percent of your income in taxes, the last dollars you earn are taxed at the 30 percent rate. And yes, you do indeed qualify for the 30 percent-plus club. In making your investment decisions, you should assume that your earnings from a certificate, or any other investment, would be your last dollars earned and therefore taxed at the highest rate applicable.

Since you are right at the 30 percent tax bracket, you would do about equally well with a one-year Treasury bill or a 1-year savings certificate. Below the 30 percent tax bracket, you'd be better off opting for something other than the savings certificates. And the higher you get above the 30 percent bracket, the more attractive the certificate would be. But if your state and municipality tax the certificates, that would make them slightly less attractive.

Q: I am in a high tax bracket — 50 percent. Would I be better off buying a tax-exempt municipal bond rather than a tax-exempt savings certificate?

A: There may well be investments — either taxable or tax-exempt — that provide a higher after-tax return than the savings certificates. But probably few of these do so at so little risk. Since the certificates are deposits insured by a Government-sponsored agency, they carry virtually no risk. For this level of risk, you probably can't do much better. If you are willing to take higher risks, there probably are other investments with greater returns after tax. But, especially where the certificates will not be subject to state or local tax, these certificates still don't look too bad.

For the sophisticated investor, the important question may be whether you want to invest in a one-year certificate. If you think interest rates are climbing, you may want to stay in a money market fund or other very short-term investments. And if you think rates are falling, you may want to put as much money as possible into investments with maturities much longer than a year.

5

Tax-Deferred Savings: The Individual Retirement Account

Saving for retirement will be more financially attractive under the new tax law. The rules are so beneficial that virtually everyone with any kind of wage or salary income should consider establishing a tax-deferred retirement account. (The new provisions are effective January 1, 1982.) "Here you've got the simplest, safest tax shelter you could have," says Herbert Paul, associate national tax director for Touche Ross. "This is a gift that everybody ought to take advantage of."

In a sweeping expansion of the eligibility requirements for tax-deferred retirement accounts, the new tax law permits people who are already covered by pension plans to establish Individual Retirement Accounts, commonly known as I.R.A.'s, as well. Self-employed people with retirement programs known as Keogh plans may also establish I.R.A.'s.

The theory behind the individual retirement account is simple. You are allowed to deduct from taxable income a portion of the money you earn, as long as the money is put into a specially designated investment account. Earnings on this account are allowed to accumulate tax-free. You do not have to pay taxes on any of these funds until you withdraw them, generally after retirement. At that point the withdrawals are subject to income taxes. If you are retired, you may well be in a lower tax bracket.

People in all tax brackets should benefit from this tax-deferred savings plan. But the higher your tax bracket, the more the Government is helping you save. Since money put in an

I.R.A. is deductible from taxable income, the "real" cost of putting $2,000 into a special retirement account is only $1,000, if you are in the 50 percent tax bracket. If you did not put $2,000 in the I.R.A., you would have had to pay a 50 percent tax on the $2,000, leaving you with only $1,000 after tax. In placing $2,000 in an I.R.A., you are out of pocket only $1,000. The advantage to people in lower tax-brackets is somewhat less.

There are some restrictions. Any money withdrawn from a tax-free retirement account before age 59½ will be subject to a 10 percent penalty. The financial institution or company that has custody of the account must report all withdrawals to the Government, so that they can be taxed.

This tax-deferred build-up to pay for retirement is in sharp contrast to the Social Security program, which individuals support with after-tax dollars. Some observers who welcome the greater incentive for personal savings point out that it could form the base for shrinking the Social Security program sometime later. "The Government's basic thrust is to say that people are going to have to save for themselves, to provide for their own retirement," says Howard Stein, chairman of the Dreyfus Corporation.

If you anticipate a tax rate after retirement as high as the rate you pay now, it probably still makes sense to establish an I.R.A. That is because money in an I.R.A. will compound faster than it would if taxes had taken a bite out of each dollar invested and each dollar earned on the investment. According to calculations by Touche Ross, if you put $2,000 a year into an I.R.A. each year for 20 years, and earned 12 percent on the funds invested, you would accumulate $160,000. Over 40 years, that sum would jump to $1.7 million. Of course, if inflation, too, continues at a high rate over those 40 years, $1.7 million will be worth considerably less than it is today. "Even if you are only putting in small amounts now, over time, because of compounding, the sums become astronomical," comments Mr. Paul, of Touche Ross. At 12 percent, the sum doubles every six years.

Despite its general appeal, the I.R.A. may create something of a dilemma for individuals who save in a company savings plan where the employer matches their own contributions, typically putting up $1 for every $2 contributed by the employee. If you participate in such a matching savings plan, where the company's contributions depend on your own contributions, then the money you put up will not count as I.R.A. contributions, warns Deborah Marx Fishman, a partner at Kwasha Lipton, the employee benefits consulting firm. "For the average employee, who does not have enough money both to establish an I.R.A. and to continue in the company savings plan, the choice of which is better is not clear-cut," she says. "The tax deduction for an I.R.A. is only a temporary thing, while the company match can be an outright gift, and the funds can be withdrawn sooner and without penalty."

How They Work

The new rules governing retirement accounts are simple. Anyone with income from wages or salaries may take up to $2,000 of that income each year and put it into a specially designated retirement account. An individual with earnings from investments — but no compensation income — would not qualify for the special tax provisions for I.R.A.'s.

The new law allows you to put as much as 100 percent of your earned income into an I.R.A., with a limit of $2,000. This means that beginning in 1982, if you earned only $2,000 and did not need that money for living expenses, you could put all $2,000 into an I.R.A. (The new tax-exempt savings certificates, which permit individuals to exclude up to $1,000 in interest from the certificates after October 1, 1981, have no connection with the I.R.A. program, and generally would not be a smart investment for an I.R.A. You should consider taking advantage of both programs, however.)

Previous rules governing retirement accounts prevented you from establishing an I.R.A. if you were covered by a company pension plan. And if you did set up an I.R.A., you could put no more than 15 percent of your income into it, up to a limit of $1,500 per person. Now, even if you are self-employed, you can put $2,000 into an I.R.A. on top of the $15,000 you can put into a Keogh plan, and you can then deduct all of the $17,000 from taxable income.

The new law, like the old, lets you set up an I.R.A. for your spouse, if your spouse does not hold a job. Contributions to the two accounts together may now total as much as $2,250 a year, and the money may be divided almost any way between the two accounts. The only restrictions are that at least $250 must be put in the account of the non-working spouse, and that no more than $2,000 may be put in either account in one year. Of course, if both spouses work, each of you may establish your own I.R.A., and each of you may make annual tax-deductible contributions of $2,000 a year.

While these accounts — and the tax exemption — are attractive, you should think hard about whether you are prepared to lock away the money until age 59½. For if you withdraw the money before then, not only would you have to pay income tax on money withdrawn, but you would also have to pay a penalty equal to 10 percent of the sums taken out early. "If you're making only $10,000 a year, you may have better things to do with your money than put it aside for 30 or 40 years," notes John W. Hamm, a tax partner at Arthur Young.

If you withdraw the money after you reach age 59½, you will still have to pay income tax on the money, but there will not be a penalty. The money may be withdrawn gradually or all at once. In fact, at age 59½, you could also choose not to withdraw any money at all, and leave your money in your account, to continue its tax-free compounding. However, you must begin to make withdrawals by the time you turn 70½.

Money withdrawn after age 70½ may also be received all at once or gradually. If it is taken out gradually, it must be withdrawn on at least as fast as a schedule that would reduce the account to zero by the time you and your spouse are expected to die. Most banks and other institutions that are custodians for such retirement accounts can supply actuarial tables to determine this period.

You may set up an I.R.A. for a year's income at any time until you file your income tax return for that year. This means, for example that you could put money into an I.R.A. for your 1982 income as late as April 15, 1983, or even later if you get an extension for filing your income tax return. Since the new provisions governing I.R.A.'s do not take effect until January 1, 1982, however, you may not set up an I.R.A. for your 1981 income in 1982 unless you qualified for such an account under the old tax law. You could, however, put money into an I.R.A. for 1982 as early as January 1, 1982.

How to Set Up an I.R.A.

While most tax matters are complicated, setting up an I.R.A. is not. It can be as easy as opening a bank account or investing in a money market fund. "It really is very easy, and by opening a special retirement account you are getting that all-crucial tax deduction," says Don Unterwood, manager for retirement plans and services at Merrill Lynch.

The only real challenge is deciding how to invest your money. There are relatively few restrictions on I.R.A.'s. The usual tax considerations, however, go by the wayside. Beyond that, the same considerations — safety, convenience, and yield — that apply to your other investments should apply to an I.R.A. "A good rule of thumb is to look for the safest investment with the highest return," recommends Mr. Paul, at Touche Ross. "Going for the highest yield is really

There are basically three restrictions on I.R.A. investments:

WHAT YOU CAN'T BUY: The funds may not be used to buy life insurance. Because money already accumulates in insurance accounts tax free, and may also escape taxation when a person dies, Congress did not want to permit yet another layer of tax deferral through an I.R.A.

COLLECTIBLES: The new I.R.A. rules penalize investments in collectibles — diamonds, art works, antiques, stamps and coins, and so forth. Beginning in 1982, any I.R.A. money that is used to buy collectibles will be considered a withdrawal from the account, and taxed. If you are not yet 59½, you will also face the penalty for early withdrawals. So stay away from collectibles.

FULL PAYMENTS REQUIRED: I.R.A. investments must be paid for in full. You may buy stocks. But do not plan to buy them — or any other investments — on margin. Nor should you count on buying real estate if it must be financed.

Most financial institutions handle the tax-deferred retirement accounts. These include banks, savings and loan associations, insurance companies, brokerage firms, and investment management companies. Many of these organizations will be able to give you a booklet describing what kind of program they offer. The new tax law also permits corporations to handle special retirement accounts for their employees, subject to the same rules that govern I.R.A.'s.

Under the old law, the bulk of the money in I.R.A.'s was in various kinds of bank deposits. But with the expansion of the I.R.A. program, brokers and mutual fund companies are expected to make a greater pitch for the money. Most of these institutions have programs with simple registration forms to create an I.R.A. "We'll have a system for people to take money already in our mutual funds and move it into an I.R.A.," Mr. Stein of Dreyfus noted.

Despite the special tax privileges given to these retirement accounts, they are easy to establish. All you need to do is to put money into some kind of savings or investment, such as a bank account or a money market fund or even a special fund managed by some employers. You may even have a special brokerage account to trade stocks and bonds, and you may direct the selections. When you set up the account, you must fill out a form provided by the bank or fund manager declaring that it is a special retirement account. Until tax time, that form and probably a small annual fee are the only features that distinguish an I.R.A. from any other savings or investment account.

It is when the tax return is filed that the real difference appears. Money placed in a special retirement account may be subtracted from earnings before income taxes are calculated. Any income earned in that account is also not taxable.

Despite the favored tax treatment, I.R.A.'s are not guaranteed or insured by the Government. If you place your money in stocks that lose value, the Government will not make up the loss. If, however, you place your I.R.A. money in investments that are already insured by the Government, such as deposits at banks and thrift institutions, they would remain insured.

Another possible alternative is to have your funds managed in a plan set up by the company you work for. Many large companies and some smaller ones are expected to offer such programs. If so, they may collect your money through payroll deductions. The money must then be placed in a plan that meets Government requirements for tax-free accumulation of funds, which might be a pension plan, profit-sharing plan, or savings plan managed by the company. "For the employee who keeps putting off establishing an I.R.A. until tax time and then has to scrape up money just to pay the taxes, payroll contributions can be a convenient way of accumulating retirement dollars," says Robert E. Wallace, a benefits adviser with Buck Consultants.

Although tax-deductible contributions to a qualified company plan are not technically known as Individual Retirement Accounts, they are subject to the same rules and for most employees accomplish the same purpose. You should examine the investment results of a plan before deciding whether you want to use it; sometimes you may have a choice among investments.

Another point in favor of an employer-managed plan, says Stanley M. Rosow, a partner at Hewitt Associates, is this: "If an employee puts his tax-deductible dollars into an employer plan, the employer can probably skip taking out withholding taxes from the money. An employee who puts money into an I.R.A. will still find withholding taxes being taken out."

The only restriction on the dollars you contribute to a company plan is that the money, known as "qualified voluntary contributions," must be designated as tax-deductible dollars. Furthermore, they may not result in any further benefit to the employee from the company. This means, for example, that if you are in a matching savings plan, where your employer contributes money if you do, you may not count those dollars as tax-deductible.

If you are unsure of how your company plan works, ask. If your dollars are matched on some basis, you may not deduct your own contributions from your taxable income. In some cases, the matching may be more generous than the tax deduction, depending on the matching rate and your tax bracket. If you can afford to put money into both a matching program and a tax-deductible retirement plan, you should probably take advantage of both.

Once you know what, if anything, your company offers in managing tax-deductible dollars, you should consider what is available elsewhere. You could ask several different companies to send information on their programs, and then talk to a sales person or account executive at the ones that seem most promising. If you are seeking information before 1982, however, you could run into some confusion. Financial firms may still be updating their materials to conform to the new law, and you may receive information pertaining to the old rules.

Among the factors you should compare are these:

KINDS OF INVESTMENTS: What types of investment opportunities does the institution offer? A bank might offer various kinds of certificates of deposit and savings accounts. A brokerage firm might permit a whole range of investments, including stocks and bonds chosen by the individual, or a mutual fund, or an investment trust.

EARNINGS AND RISKS: How much willthe money in the I.R.A. earn, and what risks are involved? Financial institutions offer different investment instruments, so the individual may want to shop around for the ones with the highest and safest returns.

FEES: What fees will be charged for setting up the I.R.A., for maintaining it, and for withdrawals? Rates schedules vary considerably, although the fees will be deductible for those individuals who itemize deductions. As of September 1981, Oppenheimer & Company, for example, charged customers $30 a year for I.R.A.'s. Merrill Lynch had a $25 fee to open an account, and then charged an annual custodial fee of $40 or 0.2 percent of assets — whichever is greater. Fidelity Management and Research charged a $10 fee for each mutual fund the I.R.A. is invested in at the end of each year. Individuals should also expect to pay normal commission and management costs.

SWITCHING FUNDS: How much movement will the institution permit among investments? You may decide that it was a mistake to have put the funds in one investment, and that you would prefer to invest in something else. The tax law gives you some flexibility, and allows you to change investments as long as you obey certain rules.

Active changes, where you take your money back and place it elsewhere, are known as rollovers. You are allowed one rollover every 12 months. In a rollover, you have up to 60 days from the time you receive your money from one I.R.A. to establish a new one, before the money is deemed a withdrawal and therefore subject to tax.

If the financial institution that is the custodian for your I.R.A. offers more than one form of investment, you can move back and forth among the different investments as often as you wish — and as often as the financial institution allows. So long as the money is not sent back to you in between investments, but remains in the custody of the financial institution, these shifts are not rollovers. Thus, you could move from stocks to bonds, or from a money market fund to an equity fund, as many times as you wish within a year, provided your I.R.A. custodian offers those choices and allows you to make such changes.

Fidelity Management and Research, for example, allows investors to move their money from one mutual fund to another, but no more than four times a year. I.R.A. money invested in certificates of deposit at banking institutions will be subject to the same penalties for early withdrawal as regular deposits. Other companies may have their own rules, either more or less liberal. If your I.R.A. money is in a certificate of deposit that carries penalties for early withdrawal, you would still be subject to those penalties if you move your money before the certificate matures.

If you decide to take advantage of the new I.R.A. rules, you should think about putting aside the money as early as you are permitted. For example, if you wanted to make a $2,000 contribution from your 1982 income, you could make it as early as January 1, 1982, or as late as April 15, 1983 (if that is when you filed your 1982 tax return). To take most advantage of the tax deferral, you should make your contribution in January. Let's say hypothetically that the $2,000 will be in a money market fund earning 18 percent interest, both before and after you put it into your I.R.A. Either way, you would earn $465 between January 1, 1982, and April 15, 1983. If the $2,000 were not in the I.R.A. for those 15½ months, you would have to pay taxes on that $465. In the 50 percent tax bracket, that would cost you an extra $232.50. So if you use an I.R.A., use it to its fullest advantage; don't waste the tax exemption.

Q: I hold two jobs. May I set up two I.R.A.'s, and deduct $4,000 from my total taxable income?

A: You may not deduct more than $2,000 from your taxable income for an I.R.A. in any one year. You may split that $2,000 among as many retirement accounts as you like. There is no limit on how many I.R.A.'s you may have, just as there is no limit on how many bank accounts or brokerage accounts you may have.

From a practical point of view, it probably makes sense to put all your money in one account for convenience, at least as long as the total sum is relatively small. As you add more money each year and your I.R.A. grows larger, you may want to divide it among two or more accounts for investment diversification.

Q: I participate in my company pension plan, and a profit-sharing plan. Can I also set up an I.R.A.?

A: Yes. Your contributions to your profit-sharing plan are made from after-tax dollars. Contributions you make to an I.R.A. are deducted from your taxable income. The new law permits no more than $2,000 of tax-deductible dollars per person each year, beginning in 1982.

Q: I would like to put my I.R.A. into a six-month money market certificate at my bank. Is that allowed?

A: Yes. Just remember that the six-month certificates require a $10,000 deposit. If you have been saving through an I.R.A. for some time, you may have enough in your account to buy a six-month certificate. But if you are just starting an I.R.A., the maximum annual investment of $2,000 will not be enough to purchase a six-month certificate.

Q: I am 73 and self-employed and still contributing to my Keogh account. But I am told that I can no longer contribute to an I.R.A. Have I misunderstood the rules for the Keogh and the I.R.A., or are they different?

A: You have understood correctly. The rules governing contributions after age 70½ do differ. In the I.R.A. you must start withdrawals by age 70½ and you may no longer make contributions after that age. In the Keogh you must start withdrawals by age 70½ but you may also continue to contribute past that age. The continued contributions can work to your advantage.

Q: When I retire, I have the option of rolling my pension funds into an I.R.A. Is there any limit on how much of my pension fund I can roll into an I.R.A. in one year?

A: No. The I.R.A. will continue to defer taxes on your pension investments. But when you finally begin to withdraw some money (as you must start doing by age 70½), you will be taxed at ordinary income rates on the funds you withdraw. If you simply take the money from the pension fund without rolling it into an I.R.A., you may be eligible to be taxed under a special "10-year forward averaging" formula.

You should calculate which method will work best for you — which method will minimize your tax payments. Among the factors you should consider are how many years you have until you reach age 70½ and what tax rates you will be paying. You might be able to get some help with the calculations from an employee benefits counselor, if your employer has one.

Q: I have heard that some I.R.A. accounts are better than others. Is there some source from which I can get data on what is offered?

A: The rules governing the I.R.A.'s are the same no matter where you put your money. What differs from one I.R.A. to the next is the choice of investments. Your choice is pretty much the same as if you were not setting up an I.R.A. and simply had $2,000 to invest. The question is, What investment do you think will show the best performance? Will stocks do better than bonds? Will money market funds outperform annuities?

One other key difference is taxes. Outside of an I.R.A., you might consider how your investment returns will be taxed before choosing an investment. Since the investment returns from an I.R.A. are not immediately subject to tax, that should no longer be a factor in your decision. If you liked stocks because their profits would be taxed at the 20 percent capital gains rate, rather than at ordinary income tax rates, that no longer matters in an I.R.A. If you try one investment for your I.R.A., and later decide you do not like it, you can change the investment, subject to certain rules.

Q: Money in an I.R.A. may not be used to buy a life insurance policy. Can I use my I.R.A. to buy an annuity from an insurance company?

A: Yes. There is no prohibition against using an insurance company for your I.R.A., only against life insurance policies. If your insurance company runs a money market fund or other mutual funds, you might consider putting your I.R.A. into these.

Q: Since I direct my own I.R.A. investments, the new law does not allow me to put money in collectibles. What is included in that category?

A: The tax law lists art works, rugs, antiques, metals, gems, stamps, coins, alcoholic beverages and any other tangible personal property specified by the Treasury Secretary.

Q: I plan to start withdrawing funds from my I.R.A. when I turn 59½. Do I have to withdraw those funds on a schedule based on my life expectancy at the time?

A: No. You can make any withdrawals you want at that point, as quickly or as slowly as you wish. Whatever funds, if any, are in the account when you turn 70½, however, must then be withdrawn on a schedule based on your life expectancy and that of your spouse.

Q: Can I withdraw funds from my I.R.A. at age 60 if I am still working?

A: Yes. But since you will have to pay income taxes on the funds you withdraw whenever you withdraw them, you may prefer to wait until you retire. At that time both your income and your tax rate are likely to be lower.

Q: If I die before I have withdrawn all of my I.R.A. funds, does the Government get them?

A: No. They will go to the beneficiary you have named, or into your estate.

6

Tax-Deferred Savings: The Keogh Account

If you are self-employed, or if you have any kind of free-lance income, the new tax law greatly expands your opportunity to accumulate tax-deferred savings for retirement, through a vehicle known as a Keogh plan.

Beginning in 1982, a self-employed person may put twice as much money into a Keogh as was previously allowed. In general, the new maximum will be $15,000 a year, up from the $7,500 permitted now. (In a specific kind of plan, known as a defined-benefit Keogh, the sums may go higher.)

"Because of the larger benefits that will be available, the Keogh will be a much more attractive vehicle, and many younger, high-income individuals who are self-employed may find that they do not gain anything by incorporating," says Michael Costello, a tax partner at the accounting firm of Laventhol & Horwath. In recent years, many high-income self-employed persons have incorporated their businesses to allow them to put aside more tax-deferred money for retirement. However, if you are in your late 50's and want to accumulate a nest egg for retirement, even the new Keogh may not allow the contributions that you could make in a corporate pension plan, Mr. Costello points out.

The Keogh, named after former Brooklyn Congressman Eugene J. Keogh, who sponsored the bill that set up the plans in 1962, is simply the self-employed individual's equivalent of a corporate pension plan. (The Keogh is also known as an H.R. 10 plan, for the number of the bill in the House of Representatives.) The rules governing Keoghs are similar to those for Individual Retirement Accounts, though there are some differences, including eligibility, contribution amounts, and permitted investments.

Moreover, as Francis M. Gaffney, national director of tax services for Main Hurdman, points out, "The Keogh is much more powerful than the Individual Retirement Account since [under the new tax law], you are limited to annual contributions of $2,000 for an I.R.A., while the Keogh permits contributions of up to $15,000 annually."

While the new law makes the Keogh more attractive than ever, it also tightens up on one privilege available to some people under the old tax law: the ability to borrow from one's Keogh account. "Beginning in 1982, self-employed people will no longer be allowed to borrow from their Keogh plans," notes Richard Reichler, a principal at Ernst & Whinney. "Previously, this restriction applied only to people whose share of a business was more than 10 percent."

Even with this provision, however, many tax specialists are urging their clients to take full advantage of the higher limits on Keoghs. The Keogh, they emphasize, is a tool available to anyone with a source of outside income from services (not from investments), even those who are also in corporate pension plans. "We recommend that directors of corporations use their income from their directorships to set up Keogh plans," Mr. Gaffney says.

The benefits are many. Since Keogh contributions are deductible from taxable income, if you place $15,000 in a Keogh, you reduce your taxable income by $15,000. In most cases, that should also move you into a lower tax bracket.

Furthermore, if you are in the 50 percent tax bracket and put $15,000 in a Keogh, you would be out of pocket by only $7,500. Had you not contributed $15,000 to a Keogh, you would have had to pay $7,500 in tax, leaving you with only $7,500 after tax. In effect, then, the Government would be putting up half of your Keogh contribution. Of course, if you are in a lower tax bracket, the Government is footing less of your bill. Another benefit is that whatever money is earned in a Keogh account is free from tax until it is withdrawn.

That allows funds to compound much more quickly than if tax were taken out each year.

Still, the money does not escape tax forever. You will be taxed on the funds as you draw them from the account. If you withdraw the money gradually, it will be taxed at ordinary income rates. If you withdraw it all at once, it can qualify for a special averaging tax rate that is sometimes more favorable.

There is one important restriction on the Keogh account. No money may be withdrawn until you are 59½ years old, although, if you are an owner of your business, withdrawals must begin by the time you turn 70½. If you pull any money out before you are 59½, you will have to pay a penalty equal to 10 percent of the sum withdrawn, in addition to paying tax on the sum you take out. If you make an early withdrawal, you will also generally be barred from making any further contributions to a Keogh for five tax years following your withdrawal. (The penalties apply to owners of unincorporated businesses and to major partners in a firm; partners with less than a 10 percent share of a business are not subject to these penalties.)

Even with these penalties, the tax-free compounding may make the Keogh a worthwhile investment vehicle, even if you do not intend to leave the money there until you turn 59½. In this case, whether you are better off using the Keogh or not using it depends on your tax bracket, the rate of return on the Keogh investments, and how long the money is left in. Remember, however, that you wold have to wait five years before being allowed to make additional contributions.

You may make contributions to Keogh plans for as long as you are self-employed. (Thus, you can be making contributions and withdrawals at the same time.) The absence of any age limit for making contributions is in contrast to the Individual Retirement Account, which bars contributions after age 70½. In both types of accounts, you may make contributions for each year at any time until you file your tax return for that year.

The amount you may contribute to a Keogh is governed by your self-employment income for the year. That means income after sales and operating expenses have been subtracted, but before taxes. Beginning in 1982, up to $200,000 of your income may be taken into account in figuring a Keogh contribution. That is double the $100,000 ceiling that now applies. You may place up to 15 percent of that self-employed income — up to the limit — in a Keogh.

There is another ceiling as well. Under the new tax law, you may not contribute more than $15,000 in any one year. That, however, is double the maximum contribution allowed under the old law. Thus, if you had $20,000 of self-employment income in 1982, you could make a Keogh contribution of $3,000 (15 percent of $20,000). But if you had $150,000 of self-employment income in 1982, you could make a contribution of only $15,000. While 15 percent of $150,000 comes to $22,500, you would be limited to the new $15,000 maximum.

The law requires that if you establish a Keogh for yourself, you must make contributions to a pension plan for all of your full-time employees as well, provided they have worked in your business for at least one year and that they are at least 25 years old. (There is an exception for employees whose pension benefits are subject to collective bargaining.) The contributions for employees must be the same percentage of their salaries as you put into your own Keogh.

There is latitude in the law, however, for you, as owner, to maximize your contribution while holding down the contributions for your employees. Assume, for example, that you have $200,000 of self-employment income in 1982. The maximum contribution you could make to a Keogh would be $15,000. But you could reach that figure in at least two ways: by taking 15 percent of the first $100,000 in income, or by taking 7.5 percent of the whole $200,000.

The only real difference in these two calculations involves the amount you would have to contribute to your employees' pension plans. If you used 15 percent to figure your own Keogh contribution, you would have to put 15 percent of the salaries of your employees into a pension plan too. But if you used 7.5 percent to figure your Keogh contribution, the contribution required for your employees would be cut in half. The law does require that if you base your contributions on more than $100,000 of your income, then contributions for employees may not total less than 7.5 percent of their salaries.

There is an exception to the $15,000 limit on contributions. If you participate in a defined-benefit Keogh, whose payout is determined by a formula based on your salary, you may make contributions that exceed the general limits. Your contributions would be based on the money needed to fund the prescribed benefits, which would be calculated according to actuarial projections.

The new law also makes a change in the penalty rules for early withdrawals. The old law said that if you made early withdrawals for any reason other than disability, you not only were subject to a 10 percent penalty charge, but you were also barred from making any new contributions to a Keogh for five years. The new law extends the exemption from the five-year restriction to persons whose Keogh plans are terminated.

Generally, each Keogh should have a custodian, usually a bank or other financial institution. "It is very important in choosing a plan that you read the fine print, particularly about your ability to transfer or withdraw funds," recommends Mr. Reichler, of Ernst & Whinney. "Some financial institutions are more restrictive than others."

You will still be free to choose your own investments, if you care to, be they stocks or bonds, bank certificates of deposit, money market fund shares, or virtually anything else that seems attractive. You can even use your Keogh to buy life insurance policies, which are not permitted in I.R.A.'s.

Deciding how to invest the money in a Keogh is similar to choosing any other set of investments. Tax considerations, however, should no longer be a factor, because earnings in a Keogh are exempt from tax. Also, since any asset placed in a Keogh that has been acquired with the help of borrowed funds will be subject to tax, you may want to avoid purchasing assets where financing would be required.

As attractive as the Keogh is, tax advisers caution that you should not place any more in a Keogh than allowed by law. There is a 6 percent penalty for any contributions beyond what is permitted. The penalty will be levied each year that there is excess money in the account. Beginning in 1982, there will be no penalty for excess contributions if you remove them from the Keogh, along with the earnings on those funds, before you file your annual tax return. While that problem could be avoided by making contributions later in the year rather than earlier, some tax advisers recommend a different strategy. "One thing people should do is to make their contributions as early as possible, so they can get their tax-free return all year," suggests Mr. Costello, of Laventhol & Horwath.

Q: The new maximum contribution for Keogh plans beginning in 1982 is $15,000. I have $30,000 of self-employment income a year. I want to put as much into a Keogh plan as I am allowed. Can I contribute $15,000?

A: The maximum allowable contribution to a Keogh beginning in 1982 is indeed $15,000. But there is also another rule that limits your Keogh contribution to 15 percent of your self-employment income. For $30,000 of income, that amounts to $4,500. So $4,500 is the most you can contribute to the Keogh.

Q: I have $200,000 of self-employment income. What is the maximum I can contribute to a Keogh?

A: Your maximum allowable contribution would be $15,000. Although 15 percent of your income amounts to $30,000, you would be held to the $15,000 limit.

Q: I have $30,000 in self-employment income and want to put as much as I can into both a Keogh and an I.R.A. What is the most I may put in each one?

A: Beginning in 1982, you may establish an Individual Retirement Account, as well as a Keogh, based on your self-employment income. The new limit on I.R.A. contributions starting in 1982 is $2,000. (The amount may not exceed your income, but it may represent as much as 100 percent of your income.) So you would be allowed to put $2,000 into an I.R.A. and another $4,500 into a Keogh. Together, those two contributions would allow you to subtract $6,500 from your taxable income. That would leave you with taxable income of $23,500 (before other deductions), not $30,000.

Q: I have a corporate pension plan and I plan to start an I.R.A. May I also have a Keogh?

A: Yes. You may have all three, starting in 1982, assuming you have self-employment income. Under the old tax law, you could have had both a Keogh and a corporate pension plan at the same time, but not an I.R.A.

Q: I earn $25,000 in my corporate salary and $30,000 of self-employment income a year. How much can I put in an I.R.A. and how much can I contribute to a Keogh?

A: You may put $4,500 into a Keogh plan (15 percent of that $30,000). Your maximum allowable contribution to an I.R.A. would be $2,000.

Q: I hold a job with a company and I also run a small business in my spare time. I have a corporate pension plan and a Keogh plan. Would I be allowed to start up two I.R.A.'s in 1982, one for my corporate salary and one for my small business income?

A: You can have more than one I.R.A., but you may not deduct more than $2,000 a year from your taxable income to put into I.R.A.'s. So if you set up more than one account, your total contributions can not exceed $2,000.

Q: If I put money into a Keogh plan, and then need it to buy a house in a couple of years, may I take the money out to buy the house?

A: The law permits you to withdraw your money whenever you want, but if you are an owner of your business or a major partner in it, it penalizes you for withdrawals made before you reach 59½. The penalty is 10 percent of the amount of money you withdraw. There is another penalty as well: You will generally be barred from making new contributions to a Keogh for five tax years following your early withdrawal. Under the old law you would have been exempted from this five-year rule if you were disabled. The new law extends the exemption to one other group of people, those whose Keogh plans have been terminated.

Q: I had a Keogh plan and withdrew my money in 1979, before I reached age 59½. Under the old tax law, I would have had to wait five years to make new contributions to a Keogh. Is this still true?

A: In general, if you withdraw money from a Keogh before age 59½, you would still be barred from making contributions to that plan for five tax years following the year you made your withdrawal. Under the old law, the only exception was for early withdrawals made because you had become disabled. The new law permits one other exception: the termination of a plan. Any early withdrawals made before January 1, 1981, would still leave you subject to the five-year waiting period provisions of the old law. The new rule applies only to withdrawals made on or after January 1, 1981.

Q: I am a doctor and have income of $150,000 a year. I have been thinking of incorporating my practice to allow me to set aside more tax-deductible pension money. Does this still make sense under the more favorable provisions for Keoghs?

A: As a general rule, younger self-employed individuals with high incomes may find they can do as well under the more generous Keogh provisions as they could under a corporate pension plan. Older self-employed individuals with high incomes will probably find they would still do better by incorporating. You should consult with a lawyer or tax accountant to decide what is best.

Q: I had borrowed from my Keogh account before the new tax law was passed. Do I need to repay that loan immediately?

A: No. You can continue to pay off the loan as scheduled. However, if you are a partner in your business, you would not be allowed to renegotiate the loan in any way after December 31, 1981.

Q: Can my Keogh plan funds be invested in collectibles, such as art works or gems?

A: You should not plan to acquire collectibles after December 31, 1981, if you have a self-directed account in which the responsibility for the investment decisions lies with you. Any collectibles you acquired would be considered withdrawals from the account. The term collectibles includes works of art, antiques, metals, gems, stamps, coins, and alcoholic beverages (such as wines).

7

The Working Spouse

Until now, the American tax system tended to penalize married couples with two incomes, by taxing them more heavily than two single individuals with the same two incomes. The new law goes a long way to offsetting that penalty, by providing a new tax deduction for married couples with two incomes. It also provides some other incentives for two-earner couples. These include better child care credits for low-income couples, and much broader tax-deferred retirement plans that can shelter from taxes the first $2,000 of your income. Lower tax rates on your income may also make working somewhat more attractive.

These tax breaks, by themselves, are unlikely to cause you to go to work if you are not already working. But if you have been torn over the possibility of working — at either a part-time job or a full-time job — the new law may tip the balance by making the economics of working more attractive.

The Marriage Penalty

The so-called marriage penalty for two-income married couples is built right into the tax tables. The penalty is greatest for couples whose incomes are relatively close together and smaller for couples with incomes farther apart. (In some instances, where a two-income couple has incomes that are very different, the married couple may sometimes pay slightly less in tax than two persons with comparable incomes who are not married. Even these married couples will be allowed to take the new tax deduction.)

Here is an example of the marriage penalty at work, where the married couple with two incomes pays higher taxes than two single individuals with the same incomes. Suppose that in 1982 you have $30,000 of taxable income (after deductions) and your spouse also has $30,000 of taxable income. The two of you filing a joint tax return would be faced with a total tax of about $17,705. (Filing separate returns would not help, either, since as a general rule, you minimize your taxes by filing a joint return. If you are married but filing individual tax returns, you would not use the same tax tables as single individuals.) Two unmarried individuals, each with $30,000 of taxable income in 1982, would have to pay a total of only $14,344 in tax, considerably less than the married couple.

The Marriage Penalty Deduction

The new law does not change the income tax tables or what these people would have to pay. What it does is to provide a special new deduction for the married couple. In 1982, a married couple will be permitted to deduct from taxable income up to 5 percent of the income (up to $30,000) of the lower-earning spouse. The maximum deduction, therefore, will be 5 percent of $30,000, or $1,500.

In 1983 and thereafter, that deduction will become more generous. The deduction will be 10 percent of the income (up to $30,000) of the lower-earning spouse. The maximum deduction, therefore, will be $3,000.

There are a few restrictions on who may take the deduction:

● It is available only to married couples filing joint tax returns.

● It may not be taken by couples working abroad who take advantage of the special provisions for sheltering income earned abroad from American taxes.

● If your only source of income is income earned by working for your spouse, and you are exempted from Social Security payments, you may not take the marital deduction. This rule is aimed at businesses that essentially consist just of one person, and are known as sole proprietorships. If your spouse's business is incorporated, for example, you would have to pay Social Security taxes on income earned working for the company and you would be allowed to take the marital deduction. The idea is that the law does not want to give you a double benefit, both by excusing you from Social Security taxes and by giving you the marital penalty deduction.

There are also some rules to keep in mind when you calculate the deduction. It is based on the earnings of the spouse with the lower income, but those earnings may not include money from pensions or annuities. The deduction is to be calculated only after other deductions, such as contributions to a tax-deferred retirement account, have been taken out of income. Thus, an individual with $10,000 in income who puts $2,000 into a tax-deferred retirement account could base the deduction on only $8,000 of income.

The deduction you get beginning in 1982 does not depend at all on how much the two of you earn together, nor on the income of the higher-earning spouse. The only determinant is the income of the lower-earning spouse. If the lower-earning spouse has taxable income of $30,000 or more, you will be able to take the maximum deduction. If the lower-earning spouse makes less than $30,000, you will be able to take only the part of the deduction that is available.

How much that deduction will be worth to you depends on what your tax bracket is. Your tax bracket is based on the couple's total income. This means that you could have two couples allowed to take the same deduction, but the deduction would be worth more to the couple with the higher total income.

Consider the case of two couples, both with the lower-earning spouse having taxable income of $30,000 in 1983. One couple has a combined taxable income of $65,000; the other has $150,000. Both couples will be allowed to take the maximum deduction, because the lower-earning spouse in both cases has income of $30,000. But, since the two couples are in different tax brackets, it will be worth more to the couple with the higher combined income.

In 1983, for example, after the individual tax cuts have

begun to take effect, $65,000 of taxable income would place a married couple in the 42 percent tax bracket. Each dollar of deduction saves 42 cents of taxes. Thus the $3,000 deduction would be worth $1,260 in tax savings to this couple. In contrast, $150,000 of taxable income would place a married couple in the 49 percent tax bracket, where each dollar of deduction saves 49 cents in taxes. The $3,000 deduction would be worth $1,470 in tax savings to the couple with more income.

While these savings will not fully offset the marriage penalty for everyone, they should lessen the inequity. Look again at the comparison above, where the husband and wife each had taxable incomes of $30,000 and paid $17,705 in taxes, while two unmarried individuals with the same two salaries paid a total of $14,344 in taxes. The married couple paid $3,361 more in taxes than the two individuals taken together. In 1982, the married couple could take a marriage penalty deduction of $1,500, well below the amount of the "penalty". In 1983, the maximum deduction will rise to $3,000. Even then, however, because the $3,000 is a tax deduction, and not a tax credit, the tax savings will amount to less than $3,000.

Child Care Credits

Couples with two working spouses may also be eligible to claim a credit for child care costs if such care is necessary to allow both spouses to work. If you are unmarried, you may also claim the credit if you pay for child care to allow you to work. To qualify for the credit, children must be under 15.

Whether you are single or married, the credit may run as high as $720 a year for one child and $1,440 for two or more children. These maximum credits, however, are available only if your income is $10,000 or less. People with higher incomes will be eligible for smaller credits. The credit may also be applied to the care of other needy dependents as well as children. Basically the same rules apply.

You are not allowed to take a credit for the the full costs of such care, only for a percentage of the expenses up to a certain limit. For people claiming the care of one dependent, no more than $2,400 in expenses may be taken into account in calculating the credit. For two or more dependents, up to

The chart below shows the maximum child care tax credit available to you according to your taxable income and number of dependents. Keep in mind that the maximum amount of expenses to which the credit may be applied is $2,400 for one child or dependent, and $4,800 for two or more. If your costs are less, calculate your credit by finding your tax bracket and the allowable percentage in the next column to the right. Then simply calculate that percentage of your costs.

If your taxable income is:	You may take a credit equal to this portion of your child care or other dependent cost:	But the credit may not exceed:	
		for one dependent	for two or more
up to $10,000	30%	$720	$1,440
$10,001 to $12,000	29%	$696	$1,392
$12,001 to $14,000	28%	$672	$1,344
$14,001 to $16,000	27%	$648	$1,296
$16,001 to $18,000	26%	$624	$1,248
$18,001 to $20,000	25%	$600	$1,200
$20,001 to $22,000	24%	$576	$1,152
$22,001 to $24,000	23%	$552	$1,104
$24,001 to $26,000	22%	$528	$1,056
$26,001 to $28,000	21%	$504	$1,008
$28,001 or more	20%	$480	$960

$4,800 in expenses may be taken into account. If you are married, the expenses you claim may not be greater than the earned income of the lower-earning spouse. If you are single, the expenses you claim may not exceed your earned income.

What percentage of those expenses you are allowed to take depends on your adjusted gross income, which is your income after your deductions have been taken but before you subtract your exemptions. People at lower amounts of adjusted gross income are allowed to take a larger percentage of their costs than people with higher incomes. If your adjusted gross income is $10,000 or less, you may claim a credit equal to 30 percent (the maximum allowed) of your expenses. That would amount to a credit of up to $720 for one child or $1,440 for two. (Thirty percent of $2,400 equals $720; thirty percent of $4,800 equals $1,440.) That percentage falls as your income grows, however. For every extra $2,000 of income, or portion thereof, the percentage of your child care costs that you may claim falls by one point.

If, for example, your adjusted gross income is between $10,001 and $12,000, you would be allowed to claim a credit of only 29 percent of your care costs, up to the same limit of $2,400 for one dependent and $4,800 for two. If your adjusted gross income is between $12,001 and $14,000, the percentage falls to 28 percent. And so on. At $28,001, however, the credit flattens out to 20 percent. The same 20 percent is available to anyone with an adjusted gross income over $28,000, whether it is $30,000 or $300,000.

Thus, only the minimum credit is available to couples with adjusted gross incomes of more than $28,000, who may take no more than $480 for one child and $960 for two or more children. The maximum credit of $1,440 is available only to couples (or single people) with adjusted gross incomes of $10,000 or less who, in order to work, must pay for the care of two dependents.

Some other rulings from the Internal Revenue Service:

● Payments to relatives who are your dependents do not qualify for the credit.

● Care for dependents other than your children must be in your home to qualify for the credit.

● The cost of a day-care center generally qualifies for the credit, but not the cost of the transportation there and back. Part of the cost of a boarding school may qualify, but not the amounts that cover tuition or food.

● Married people must file a joint return to qualify for the credit.

● If you are divorced, you may claim the child care credit in any year in which you have custody of the child longer than your former spouse, even if you do not claim the child as your dependent. If your spouse had custody for most of the year, you may not take the child care credit, even if you had child care expenses that enabled you to work.

● If you are a full-time student for at least five months of the year while your spouse works, you may be eligible for the credit if you must pay for the care of a child or other dependent. Since the student does not have an income to use in calculating the credit, the Government provides a figure.

While the child care credit may not seem to amount to much, particularly if your incomes are not below $10,000, do not dismiss it. Remember, it is a credit, rather than a deduction, so the whole amount comes directly off of your taxes.

Tax-Deferred Retirement Accounts

Another potential advantage for couples in the new law is the tax-deferred retirement account, known as the Individual Retirement Account, or I.R.A.. These accounts are not entirely new. What the tax law does is to make everybody with any earned income eligible to establish such an account, beginning in 1982. Before, if you worked in a company with a pension plan that covered you, you were not allowed to set up a tax-deferred retirement account.

Such accounts should be useful to anyone, either married or single. But they are expected to be a special boon to many couples, particularly couples where one spouse works only part-time or earns a relatively small salary. That is because the new law changes the rules governing such accounts so that they should be more useful to people with relatively small amounts of income.

"One of the problems that used to arise when a spouse went to work and earned a relatively small amount of money, is that after tax, there just wasn't much left, because it was added to the income from the principal wage earner and taxed at a higher rate," explains Richard Reichler, a partner at the accounting firm of Ernst & Whinney. "Under the new rules for Individual Retirement Accounts, the first $2,000 of earnings can be free of taxes. So working should be much more attractive for a spouse who wants to take a part-time job." Of course, once you put the money into an I.R.A., it is forced savings, rather than spendable income.

Under the new rules, anyone with earned income may set up an I.R.A. beginning in 1982. The law allows people to place as much as 100 percent of their incomes — up to a limit of $2,000 — in an investment account whose earnings will not be taxed until they are withdrawn after the wage-earner turns 59½. (There is a penalty for withdrawals made before age 59½.) The money placed in the account will also not be subject to income taxes until withdrawn after age 59½.

Previously, if you had earned income and were not covered by a pension plan, you could have set up an I.R.A. However, you could have placed no more than 15 percent of your income into the account, up to a maximum of $1,500. Therefore, if you had income of $3,000, you could have put no more than $450 into the account. That meant you could only protect the first $450 of your earnings from taxes. To many people, that might not have seemed worth the bother. (Of course, if the $3,000 were your only income, you probably wouldn't be putting any into savings. At that income level, you also would not be subject to Federal income taxes, so you would not need to consider an I.R.A.)

Under the new law, however, there is no percentage limit on your contribution. There is still a ceiling on annual contributions, but it has been raised to $2,000 from $1,500 per person. Thus, if you have income of $3,000, you would be allowed to put as much as $2,000 into an I.R.A. after 1981.

Couples with relatively low total incomes may not be able to afford to put this much into savings, especially savings that may not be drawn upon until age 59½. They also may be subject to such low Federal income tax rates that the tax-exemption does not achieve very much. But for couples where one spouse makes a high income, placing them in a high tax-bracket, the second income, no matter what size it is, disappears in taxes anyway. The I.R.A. is an easy way to protect the first $2,000 of that second income from taxes. This couple is also probably in a better position to be able to put some money into long-term savings.

Yet another benefit to be considered if you are deciding whether or not to hold a job is the new lower income tax rates, which will be phased in over three years, starting October 1, 1981. Of course the new rate will apply to all wage-earners, single or married. But either way, they will permit you to keep a greater portion of your wages and give less to the Government. By the end of the phase-in period, you will be paying taxes that are about one-quarter lower than they otherwise would have been.

Q: I earn $40,000 and my spouse earns $45,000. How do I calculate the marriage penalty deduction?

A: The deduction is based on the income of the lower-earning spouse, in your case, $40,000. If you are going to put any money into a tax-deferred retirement account, you would subtract that amount from your income before calculating the marriage penalty deduction. With the maximum contribution to a retirement account, $2,000, that would still leave you with $38,000 of taxable income. But since no more than $30,000 of income may be used in calculating the marriage penalty deduction, you could only take a deduction equal to 5 percent of $30,000, or $1,500.

Q: Both my spouse and I work. I earn $20,000 and my spouse earns $25,000. I plan to put $2,000 into an I.R.A. How much of a marriage penalty deduction may I claim?

A: If you make a $2,000 contribution to a tax-deferred retirement account, you would only be allowed to base your deduction on $18,000 of income: your total earnings less your I.R.A. contribution. In 1982, your deduction would be 5 percent of $18,000, or $900. In 1983, if your incomes were still the same and you made the same I.R.A. contribution, your deduction would be 10 percent of $18,000, or $1,800.

Q: If making a contribution to a tax-deferred retirement account means the deduction we get for the marriage penalty is smaller, would I be better off not putting money into the tax-deferred retirement account?

A: That is an individual decision. Every dollar put into a tax-deferred retirement account is a deduction of a full dollar from your taxable income. In 1982, the marital deduction only lets you deduct 5 percent of each dollar you earn from your taxable income, with certain further limits. Therefore, you get more bang for your buck by making a retirement account contribution, even if it reduces the marital deduction you can take. Although you will eventually have to pay taxes on the money you place in a retirement account, contributions to such an account are probably wise if you do not need the money to spend and can afford to save it. On the other hand, if you have heavy spending needs now, the extra tax savings generated by the marital deduction would give you more cash immediately.

This difficult choice is not a problem if the taxable income of the lower-earning spouse is greater than $32,000. Then you can still take advantage of the tax-deferred retirement account — the $2,000 deduction — and take the maximum marriage penalty deduction — 5 precent of taxable income of $30,000.

Q: I make $10,000 and my spouse makes $60,000, the same total as a married couple where the husband and wife each make $35,000. It appears that we will get a smaller marriage penalty deduction than the other couple, although we both have the same total incomes. Is that correct?

A: Yes. The deduction you are allowed to take as relief from the marriage penalty is based on the income of the lower-earning spouse, not on the couple's total income. Therefore, if you had $10,000 of income in 1982, you would be allowed to take a deduction of $500: 5 percent of $10,000. The other couple, where the husband and wife earn $35,000 each, would be allowed a deduction of $1,500: 5 percent of $30,000, which is the maximum amount of income that may be used in the calculation.

Q: My spouse and I pay almost $4,000 more in taxes than an unmarried couple with the same two incomes we have. But our marriage penalty deduction is only $1,500. After taxes, that deduction saves us only $750 in taxes. That means we are still paying $3,250 more in taxes than the other couple. Isn't the deduction supposed to wipe out the penalty of the extra $4,000 that we pay in taxes?

A: The marriage penalty deduction is supposed to provide relief, but is not necessarily meant to offset the penalty completely.

Q: My husband and I live abroad and we both work. Will we be eligible to take the marriage penalty deduction?

A: Probably not. If either one of you makes use of the rules that protect your foreign earned income from American taxes, you could not also take the marriage penalty deduction.

Q: I am single and have an income of $21,000. I have one child and I pay someone $4,000 a year to watch the child so I can work. How much of a child care credit may I take on my taxes?

A: Child care expenses of up to $2,400 for one child may be taken into account in calculating your tax credit. Since you make $21,000, you may take a credit equal to 24 percent of your costs up to $2,400, for a credit of $576.

Q: I am single and earn $10,000 a year, and therefore can take a 30 percent credit on up to $2,400 in child care expenses. But I pay only $2,000 for someone to care for my one child. Can I take the maximum credit of $720 anyway?

A: No. If you spent $2,400 on care, you could take a credit of 30 percent of $2,400, or $720. But since you only pay $2,000, your tax credit would be 30 percent of $2,000, or $600.

Q: We pay $8,000 for someone to watch both our three-year-old son and my ninety-year-old mother while my spouse and I both work. I earn $20,000 and my spouse makes $30,000. How much of a tax credit may we claim?

A: You have two dependents being cared for, so you may use expenses of up to $4,800 as a basis for calculating the care credit. Since your combined income is $50,000, you may take a credit for 20 percent of the expenses up to that $4,800 ceiling. Thus, your credit is 20 percent of $4,800, or $960.

Q: My spouse started a business, and I work in the business about 20 hours a week, earning $15,000 a year. Are we entitled to take the marriage penalty deduction? May I contribute to a tax-deferred retirement account?

A: If the business is incorporated, or if there are several partners who own the business together, then you may take the marital deduction. But if the business is unincorporated and is owned solely by your spouse, then you may not take the deduction.

As for the tax-deferred retirement account, you would be allowed to contribute to that no matter what kind of business it was and no matter who owned it.

Q: I work part-time for my spouse, who is the sole owner of an unincorporated business. In that job I earn $15,000 a year. But I also work part-time at another job that pays me $10,000 a year. May I take the marital deduction?

A: Yes, but only the job where you do not work for your spouse may be taken into account. If you are the lower-earning spouse, then the deduction would be based on your income of $10,000 (not $25,000). In 1982, the deduction would amount to 5 percent of $10,000, or $500. In 1983, that would rise to 10 percent of $10,000, or $1,000.

8

Second Incomes: Small Businesses

There are no provisions in the new tax law tailored specifically for persons with second jobs or outside income. But if you freelance, or own a second home that you rent to others, or if your hobby has turned into a part-time vocation, the new law is peppered with measures that could help lower your taxes.

These new tax provisions also make this a particularly opportune time to start a business. While small businesses, specifically, received only limited tax breaks under the new law, many of the measures aimed at helping all business would be as applicable to a small business as to a giant corporation.

The relevant provisions range from faster write-offs for new plant and equipment to lower tax rates for very small businesses. The lower individual income tax rates and more liberal rules for tax-free retirement accounts should also help increase the amounts you can save from your earnings. Taken individually, these measures may not seem to save many tax dollars. But added together, the new provisions should make it more worthwhile to develop a second source of income or to take an avocation seriously. "There is no question that the new law helps second-income-type situations," says Herbert Paul, associate national tax director at Touche Ross.

How much these measures help the economy depends largely on how people respond to them. If many people view the lower tax rates as an incentive to earn more income, the added effort could boost economic activity. The economy could also show gains if people begin to report income they would otherwise not have reported because taxes were too high. The increasing phenomena of an underground economy — unreported income from activities such as second jobs, small businesses, illegal operations, and business conducted in cash — was one of the targets of the new tax law. It was felt that by holding tax rates down, people might be more likely to report their income than to risk being caught because they hadn't reported it. The possibilities for second incomes are many. The gardener who has been yearning to build a greenhouse could sell exotic flowers to friends to decorate their homes. The photographer who brings a bagful of cameras to every gathering could sell photographs. The cook who specializes in nouvelle cuisine with an Oriental flourish could cater meals for income.

Even if such sidelines do not amount to enough income to live on, they will generate some cash. And by using the new law to its fullest advantage, people should legally be able to keep greater amounts of that money than they would have otherwise. "More generous tax deductions will be available," Leon M. Nad, a national tax partner at Price Waterhouse, says. "But you have to keep in mind that they may be used only to offset income from the business. The only hitch is that people may find they have more tax deductions than they have income."

If you run a small business or are thinking of starting one, you should be looking at these provisions in the new law that could reduce your taxes:

FASTER DEPRECIATION: The new law says that most property used in a business may be written off over periods of three, five, ten, or fifteen years. This allows you to recover the cost of most property more quickly than under the old law. A light truck used in a business, for example, can now be written off in three years. An agricultural or horticultural structure can be depreciated in five years. Previously, notes Steven J. Leifer, a partner at Ernst & Whinney, the tax law allowed a variety of choices for selecting a depreciation period, but most of them tended to be longer and more complicated than under the new rules.

CORPORATE TAXES: The tax rates for corporate incomes below $50,000 will decline. The reductions are relatively small, and they are effective for only two years, but they will save some tax dollars. The first $25,000 of income, which is now taxed at 17 percent, will be taxed at 16 percent in 1982 and at 15 percent in 1983. Income between $25,000 and $50,000, now taxed at 20 percent, will be taxed at 19 percent in 1982 and at 18 percent in 1983. Income above $50,000 but below $100,000 is also taxed at rates well below the 46 percent corporate income tax rate, but those rates are not being changed, even temporarily. Note, however, that the lower tax rates on business income make tax deductions less valuable than they are at higher tax rates. Each dollar of deduction is worth 46 cents to a business in the 46 percent tax bracket, but only 16 cents to a business in the 16 percent tax bracket.

PERSONAL TAXES: Persons whose side businesses are not incorporated and who pay tax at ordinary income rates will benefit from the 23 percent cut in personal tax rates that will be phased in over three years, beginning October 1, 1981.

RETIREMENT ACCOUNTS: There are more generous provisions for tax-deferred retirement accounts for the self-employed. Beginning in 1982, an individual who is self-employed may put up to 15 percent of his income — up to a limit of $15,000 — into a tax-deferred retirement account known as a Keogh plan, or an H.R. 10 plan. Whatever amount is put into a Keogh may be deducted from taxable income. Currently, the limit on contributions to a Keogh is $7,500. People with self-employment income may put money into Keogh plans, even if they are also participating in a corporate pension plan and have established their own Individual Retirement Accounts as well.

CAPITAL GAINS: If a business becomes big enough to sell, a sizable portion of the selling price could be treated as capital gains. If the business has been incorporated, the sale of the stock would all count as capital gains. The new law reduces the maximum tax rate on capital gains to 20 percent from 28 percent, for all transactions after June 9, 1981. This permits the owner of a small business to keep even more of the proceeds.

All of these provisions could make running a small business more lucrative, and there are other opportunities, as well. One approach, suggested by several tax experts, involves employing your spouse in the business, especially if your spouse is not otherwise employed. "The job need not be anything more than typing or bookkeeping, but it must be a legitimate job," explains Mr. Paul, of Touche Ross. "By giving the second spouse an income, you can take greater advantage of the Individual Retirement Accounts, you may be able to use the marriage penalty relief, and, if you have young children, you can take advantage of the child care credit." Of course, all of these benefits would also accrue to any couple with two incomes, not just to those where the second spouse works for the first.

One caution: if you are working for your spouse in an unincorporated business owned solely by your spouse, then your income from that business may not count toward the marriage penalty deduction under the new tax law. You would already be exempted from paying Social Security tax, and Congress did not want to give a double benefit here. However, you would still be allowed to set up an Individual Retirement Account and could qualify for the child care credits.

Getting used to the new provisions, and particularly the new rules governing accelerated depreciation, could take some doing. This is probably one area where consulting with an accountant or other tax specialist would be particularly helpful. If you are running a small business, however, understanding the new provisions will be worth the effort.

Consider the example of the purchase of a second home that costs $100,000, and is then rented out. You will benefit in two ways under the new law. The rent you charge on the house will be taxed at a lower rate. If you were in the top tax bracket paying 70 percent taxes, the new top rate will be 50 percent starting in 1982. If you were not in the top tax bracket, your tax rate will still decline under the across-the-board tax cuts that will be phased in over three years.

As a landlord, you will also benefit from the faster depreciation rules in the new tax law. Under the new law, you can depreciate the house over 15 years. (The new depreciation rules apply only to properties bought or placed in service in 1981 or later.) If you depreciate the house on a straight line basis, you could write off, or deduct, one-fifteenth of $100,000 — or $6,667 — each year. Under the old law, you might have had to depreciate the house over 30 years or longer, giving you deductions much smaller than what you could take now, perhaps $3,333 or less. So in the first five years alone, you would have accumulated more than $16,000 in tax deductions under the new law that you would not have gotten until much later under the old law.

Of course, under both the old law and the new law as well, you could take even faster write-offs by taking accelerated depreciation rather than straight line deprcciation. The new law still gives considerably greater opportunities for faster writeoffs if you elect the accelerated methods, than the old law did.

Suppose that at the end of 15 years, you found you could sell your house for $300,000. Under the new law, your profits would be taxed at a lower rate, so you would keep more of the gain. Since you have depreciated the whole cost of the house over 15 years, you will be taxed on the amount of depreciation — $100,000 — plus the $200,000 profit on the house. Since the property is residential, and since you have taken straight-line depreciation, all of the depreciated amount will be taxed at a capital gains rate, as will the $200,000 profit. Under the new tax law, the maximum capital gains rate is only 20 percent, down from 28 percent. Thus, you would pay $60,000 in taxes under the new law, rather than the $84,000 you would have paid under the old law.

In the same example, if you had chosen to take accelerated depreciation, part of the amount that you had depreciated might have been subject to ordinary income tax rates rather than capital gains rates when you sold the house. The amount that would be treated as ordinary income would be the extra depreciation you had taken beyond what you would have gotten under straight-line depreciation. Of course, if you hold the house long enough, straight-line depreciation would catch up with your accelerated method, and there would be no excess subject to ordinary income tax rates.

If you owned a small office building or other commercial property, the benefits from the new tax law would be similar. The main difference would be on the final tax on what had been depreciated. Any amount taken under accelerated depreciation would be entirely subject to ordinary income tax, rather than capital gains. But if you had used straight-line depreciation, the whole amount would be taxed at the capital gains rate.

Other types of businesses would also benefit from the faster writeoffs under the new tax law. Most machinery can now be depreciated in only five years. This would include not only the fixtures at your local supermarket, but also pots and pans and other equipment you might use in a catering business. In the past, you might have debated with the Internal Revenue Service over how long the useful life of your equipment really would be, but now you can fall back on the new tables in the tax law. The tables do not list in detail each and every piece of property that you may want to write off, but an accountant should be able to tell you readily which of the new categories your property fits into.

The new law also spells out various schedules of accelerated depreciation that you may use if you like. Since the Government will be increasing the amount of acceleration you may take over the next few years, be sure to consult the tables for the correct year before doing any calculations.

One other potential boon to the business run out of the home is the ability to write off some of the costs of your house. The new tax law did not make any changes in this area. But some recent court cases have led to an easing in the previously rigid guidelines. Now, so long as the room is the principal place of business for your business, it may be written off. Nor does the space have to be an entirely separate room. If it is a clearly segregated area, it may qualify.

"Your writeoffs may not work out to be as dramatic as they sound," cautions Mr. Paul of Touche Ross, but he notes that they could add up to several hundred dollars each year.

He offers an example where you have bought a 10-room house for $100,000, with a 25-year mortgage. You might write off one room, with a value of $10,000, over 25 years. Each year, you could take a deduction of $400. Or, under the faster depreciation rules, you might write off the room over 15 years, for an annual deduction of $667 against your business income. Your tax savings, then, will amount to even less than the $667, because it is a deduction, rather than a tax credit.

As small as this saving may be, it underlines the importance of scanning the whole new law and using all of the measures that you can. You should not be discouraged if there is no provision that directly applies to your situation. You should be ready to use some creativity. It is after you pull together a variety of measures in the new law that the real benefits start to add up.

Q: I have my own business, and have equipment that I have already begun to depreciate. Can I switch to the new, faster depreciation schedules permitted by the new tax law?

A: No. The new depreciation schedules apply only to property purchased or put into service in 1981 or later.

Q: I ordered a new machine on December 15, 1980, and paid for it then. But I did not receive it until January 15, 1981. Will it qualify for the new depreciation rules?

A: Yes, since you put the machine into service in 1981.

Q: I am planning to set up a business, and have to buy a variety of equipment, including a desk and chair, a small computer, and some specialized machinery. How do I know how fast I can depreciate all of my different equipment?

A: The new tax law sets out categories for depreciation, dividing things into periods of three years, five years, ten years and fifteen years. You would do best to consult with a tax expert, such as an accountant or a lawyer, regarding the specific periods for your assets.

The following general guidelines, however, have been set out in the new tax law: The three-year class includes automobiles, light trucks, some special tools, and equipment used for research and experimentation. The five-year category included most machinery and furniture, some bulk storage facilities, some properties used in mining, manufacturing, communications or transporation, and agricultural and horticultural structures. The ten-year class includes some public utility properties, some coal-fired boilers and burners, and railroad tank cars. The fifteen-year class basically includes real estate and some public utility properties.

Q: I am starting my new business somewhat slowly, and do not expect to have much income from it for a couple of years. Can I depreciate my business equipment more slowly than the classes specified in the new tax law, so that I can take them when I have more income to deduct them against?

A: Yes, you can depreciate properties more slowly than the three-, five-, ten-, and fifteen-year periods. But if you choose a longer period, you must use straight-line depreciation; you may no longer elect an accelerated formula.

The new law sets out the longer optional depreciation periods (called recovery periods) that you may use. A three-year item, for example, could also be depreciated over five years or twelve years, on a straight-line basis. An item that would qualify for a five-year writeoff could also be depreciated, instead, over twelve years or twenty-five years. If, however, you elect the longer depreciation period, any other property you place in service in the same year that falls into the same category must also be written off over the same, longer period. The exception to this is real estate, which may be decided property by property.

Q: Under the old tax law, we have been depreciating a building on a component by component basis, with different periods applying to the roof, the electrical system, the plumbing, and so forth. May we also do this under the new tax law?

A: A building that is being depreciated on a component basis can continue to be treated on this basis. New buildings may not be handled this way. One exception: If you make a "substantial improvement" to an existing building, you may depreciate the improvement separately from the rest of the building.

9

Estate and Gift Taxes

Of all the tax cuts provided in the new tax law, among the most generous are the rules governing estates and gifts. They will exempt all but a handful of estates from taxes altogether, and save Americans millions of tax dollars.

Probably the most significant alteration in the estate tax rules is the provision — effective in 1982 — that will allow you, if you are married, to give everything to your spouse completely tax-free. Aside from its sizable economic impact for people with taxable estates, the measure could simplify estate planning considerably.

Congress adopted the new estate tax rules to redress the problems of inflation, which has pushed estates into ever higher tax brackets. Because the estate tax, like the income tax, is progressive, estates that mushroom with inflation are hit with higher tax rates. But as tax advisers dissect the new law and formulate financial strategies for their clients, they are beginning to recognize the social consequences of the new measure as well.

The unlimited marital deduction for spouses, for example, could pose some ticklish questions for couples deciding how to divide their properties while they are alive and how to design their estates for after they are dead. Existing tax laws have led people to follow certain practices, such as putting insurance policies in each other's names (and still paying the premiums), to avoid paying tax on the proceeds after death.

Under the new law, however, there is no longer any tax

motivation for such sharing. Tax experts predict that individuals are more likely to begin holding property in their own names, making it potentially easier to keep in case of divorce. "A person may find it difficult to get back an insurance policy that has already been placed in someone else's name," notes Peter Elinsky, a tax specialist at Peat, Marwick, Mitchell. But, he says, "There is no longer any reason to give an insurance policy to a spouse. And by keeping it, you retain control over it."

Yet another concern voiced by many tax advisers is that people may bequeath all of their money to their spouses, neglecting their children, in order to escape estate taxes. If the surviving spouse remarries, or fights with the children, the children may then receive none of the family estate. "Letting all the money go tax-free to a spouse has obvious social implications," says David S. Rhine, a tax specialist at Seidman & Seidman. "It means that many estates are going to be given entirely to the spouse and not at all to the kids."

The new law is also expected to shift patterns of personal giving in ways that could have broad implications both for families and for nonprofit organizations that depend on charitable contributions. Experts predict that this inter-spouse marital deduction could markedly reduce the sums individuals are willing to leave to charities and other non-profit institutions. This would occur just as these institutions are seeing grants and other funding from the Federal Government being cut. Under existing law, only half of a sizable estate can be left to a spouse tax-free. That has led many people to use some or all of the rest of their money to make contributions, thus avoiding estate tax on these funds.

"Planned-giving specialists feel that giving through bequests will diminish by 50 to 75 percent," says Brian O'Connell, president of Independent Sector, an alliance of foundations and others interested in private giving. "Until now, a potential donor might have decided whether to give to his favorite charity or to Uncle Sam. Beginning in 1982, the choice will be whether to give to a favorite charity or a spouse."

Of course, there are other changes in the new estate tax

rules that will also have an important impact, both economically and socially. For example, once it is fully phased in, in 1987, the new law will make all taxable estates of $600,000 or less entirely exempt from Federal taxes, no matter who inherits them. Before the new law, estates had been taxable once they exceeded $175,625. The new law will also lower the maximum tax rate on estates to 50 percent by 1985, from 70 percent. These measures, which will benefit the more well-to-do, are expected to increase the concentration of wealth in America. Federal tax analysts estimate that after all the new estate tax provisions have been phased in, fewer than five estates out of a thousand will owe any estate taxes, compared with about twenty-eight out of a thousand now. And those that do will pay substantially lower amounts.

A complicating factor is the variety of estate and inheritance tax laws in different states, many of which will not change under the new Federal act. In many states, such taxes are relatively nominal compared to the Federal taxes. An estate plan that avoids Federal taxation, however, may still be subject to taxes at the state level.

It is the new Federal rules on the tax-free transfer of assets to a spouse that are exciting the most debate among tax advisers. For while the rules themselves are fairly straightforward, the strategies that will bring the greatest benefits are less clear. At first glance, it might appear best to leave all of an estate to a spouse. It will soon be one of the simplest and surest ways to escape estate taxes completely. Some experts think that makes good sense. But others are not so sure. "That really ignores what happens when the surviving spouse dies," notes Mr. Rhine of Seidman & Seidman. "If the husband dies and leaves his entire estate to his wife, then her estate may be subject to increased taxes when she dies."

What some tax advisers are suggesting, instead, is that people give away more through tax-free gifts during their life time, taking advantage of the newly raised limits for such gifts, or that they leave some of the estate to children or other people rather than all to the spouse. Then there is less of a potential estate tax problem when the surviving spouse dies. Unless the surviving spouse remarries, the estate of the survivor could be subject to tax if it exceeds his allowable lifetime gift exclusion. Gift-giving by both the first spouse and the surviving spouse can help insure that the second estate will not be taxed.

If it is deemed desirable for the surviving spouse to have the use of the full estate, experts suggest that part of it can be put into a trust, with the income to go to the surviving spouse until death, and then be given outright to the children or other beneficiaries. The assets in trust could still be covered by the lifetime allowance for gifts and bequests.

Others say, however, that the prospect of the extra taxes when the surviving spouse dies is really not too significant. "The worst thing that could happen is that you would increase the marginal tax rate on the estate from 37 percent [the lowest marginal estate tax rate, beginning in 1986] to 50 percent [the highest marginal estate tax rate, beginning in 1985]," says Mr. Elinsky of Peat, Marwick. But in the meantime, you might have deferred taxes for 10 years and had the use of that money. In determining transfers of property, you should consider the tax treatment, but it should not be the only motivation."

Tax advisers also suggest that, even with the tax-free marital bequest, individuals should consider rearranging their properties while they are alive to save some capital gains taxes on assets that have appreciated. For example, under the new tax code, it would usually be more desirable to inherit a house from a spouse than to have been the owner or partial owner. That is because any asset left to a spouse in an estate would be valued for tax purposes at its market price at the time of the person's death, rather than at its original purchase price, which was probably lower. Thus, when the item is eventually sold, the profit would be smaller for tax purposes, and the taxes would be less.

The catch is that such transfers, which one expert calls the "double-deathbed technique," must occur more than a year before the death of the spouse who is to bequeath the property. "The only real risk is if your spouse decides to give the assets to someone else," Mr. Elinsky says.

Three Rules Governing Bequests and Gifts

Before you start drawing up your estate plan, you should understand the three basic rules that now govern what can be given away free of Federal tax, either before or after death. All are effective beginning in 1982. (Laws governing bequests and gifts at the state level must also be taken into account.)

WHAT SPOUSES GET: Estates and gifts given to spouses will be completely free from Federal tax, through the "free" marital transfer." This is a major change from the old law, which allowed the surviving spouse to inherit up to $250,000, or half of the estate, whichever was larger, without paying Federal estate tax. The old law also used to limit the amount that could be transferred tax-free from spouse to spouse while both were living.

GIFTS TO OTHERS: Annual gifts of up to $10,000 per recipient will be tax-free. That means a person with two children and two grandchildren could give them — or any other four persons — a total of $40,000 each year, free of Federal gift taxes. For a couple, that sum would double, to $80,000. Under the old law, the annual limit was $3,000 per recipient.

LIFETIME ALLOWANCE: The lifetime allowance for tax-free gifts or bequests that do not fall into either of the other two categories will be raised to $225,000 in 1982, from the current level of $175,000. It will then be increased further each year: to $275,000 in 1983, $325,000 in 1984, $400,000 in 1985, $500,000 in 1986, and $600,000 in 1987. After it reaches $600,000 in 1987, it levels out. (These sums do not include charitable contributions, which are not subject to any estate or gift tax.) The sum can be used bit by bit or all at once, and applies both to lifetime gifts and to bequests. So an individual who had given away $50,000 during his lifetime, over and above the $10,000 gifts permitted annually, would be allowed to leave $550,000 tax-free to anyone on his death in 1987 or later. But he would not be allowed to leave the full $600,000 tax-free because he had already used up $50,000 of the tax-free allowance.

The first step in planning is simply to figure out what each person owns, what estate planners call the gross estate.

All that involves is adding up the various assets: the house and other real estate, investments, bank accounts and money market fund shares, life insurance, and other property.

Using the size of the estate as a guideline, estate planners have begun to develop some new rules of thumb that take the new tax provisions into account. Most of their examples assume a couple with children, and possibly some grandchildren, since that represents the bulk of their clients. The planners caution, however, that there is no plan that will fit everybody, since each situation can vary so much from the next.

Case I: An Estate of Less Than $600,000

The simplest case involves a couple with property worth less than the lifetime allowance for tax-free gifts: only $225,000 in 1982, but $600,000 in 1987. Tax advisers point out that while these numbers may sound large, the rapid inflation in house prices has thrust many families who do not think of themselves as wealthy into these ranges.

Such a couple can handle its estate in almost any way, without having to be concerned about estate or gift taxes. If the husband dies first and leaves all of his estate to his wife, none of it will be taxed. If the wife then dies and leaves all of her property to her children, it will still escape taxes. This is, of course, provided the sum still is less than the allowance for tax-free gifts, which in 1987 would be $600,000.

Even if the husband had given some money outright to the children, the bequest would have been tax-free, because it would all have fallen within the lifetime gift exclusion.

Perhaps the only other consideration such a couple might want to take into account, if it owned a house, would be in whose name the house should be held. In this case, since the house falls within the lifetime gift exclusion, there would be no estate taxes on it. But if the couple planned well, capital gains taxes on the profit from selling the house after one of them died might also be reduced, if not avoided altogether.

The key to reducing capital gains taxes on a house or other asset that has appreciated (such as stocks or gems) is to receive it through an estate. Then, no matter what the price of the asset when purchased, the person who inherits it does so (for tax purposes) at the market value at the time it is inherited. Under the old tax law, if a couple owned a house jointly and the husband died, the entire value of the house would most likely have been included in his estate, unless the wife could show she had contributed to its purchase price. If the house had been placed entirely in the estate, then the wife would automatically have inherited the house at market price. Under the new tax law, however, the wife is considered to own half of the jointly owned property, and would receive only half of it through the estate; it would be valued at a current market price. The half she already owned would still be valued at the original purchase price, so that if she later decided to sell the house, she would be faced with a larger profit for tax purposes.

Take the case of a jointly owned house that was purchased for $50,000 and is valued at $200,000 when the husband dies. If the wife sold the house for $200,000, there would be a profit of $150,000, and there would be capital gains tax on half of it, or $75,000. If her husband had owned the entire house in his name when he died, and left it to her in his estate, she would not have had to pay any capital gains tax when she sold it since — for tax purposes — she would have acquired it for $200,000 and sold it for $200,000.

Of course, if the wife were 55 years or older, she could then use the one-time provision that allows those 55 and older to exclude from taxes the profits on selling their homes. Currently they can exclude up to $100,000 of profit. Beginning in 1982, they will be allowed to exclude $125,000.

Case II: An Estate of $600,000 to $1,200,000

Planning for a couple with property greater than the lifetime gift exclusion is slightly more complicated, estate planners say. Most of them have begun to focus on the maximum exclusion of $600,000 that will be reached in 1987. So they look next at couples with property valued at more than $600,000, but less than $1,200,000. "A couple with more than $600,000 but less than $1,200,000 has to be very careful," says Mr. Rhine, of Seidman & Seidman. "If the estate is properly structured, the couple can completely escape taxes in leaving money for the next generation. Or they could pay as much as $235,000 in estate taxes."

Consider the case of a couple with $1,000,000 in property. The first spouse — no matter how much of the $1,000,000 was in his name — could still leave everything tax-free to the second spouse. But if the second spouse died in 1987 or later, with the $1,000,000 in property still intact, only $600,000 — the maximum lifetime gift allowance — could be left free to any heirs. (Of course, if the surviving spouse had remarried, the free marital exclusion could come into play once again.) The other $400,000 would be subject to estate taxes.

One way of minimizing the taxes, estate planners say, would be for the couple, while they were still alive, to give away $400,000 of their $1,000,000 in property, through annual gifts to their heirs, up to the sums permitted annually (beginning in 1982) of $10,000 per recipient. With two children and two grandchildren, the couple could give up to $80,000 a year, transferring as much as $400,000 to the next generation tax-free, if they wished. You are not limited to making such gifts to your heirs. If you have none, or even if you do, you may still give your money to anyone you care to. The heirs do not receive special consideration under the estate and gift tax laws.

"There are several tax reasons for giving gifts before you die," notes Mr. Rhine. "The income that accumulates on the property is out of your estate. The appreciation on the property is out of your estate. And finally, both the income and the appreciation may be taxed at lower rates if the property is given to someone in a lower tax bracket than you are in."

"But," cautions Marvin Brockman, a tax partner at David Berdon in New York, "the effort to diminish the second estate for estate tax purposes has to be coupled with the question of what the surviving spouse needs to live on. You don't necessarily want to give away everything."

One answer to this, estate planners say, might call for the first spouse — let's say it's the husband — to leave $600,000 to his wife — the amount the wife could then leave to the heirs tax-free after 1986. The remainder of the $1,000,000 in property — $400,000 — could be put in a trust whose income would go to the wife for life. On the death of the wife the money in the trust would go to the heirs.

Under the new law, the husband could have given all of the money, including the $400,000 bequest, to his wife through the new unlimited marital deduction. However, he also has the option of not including the $400,000 in the marital deduction, but including it under his lifetime unified gift and bequest exclusion. The trust could be considered a bequest to the heirs from the husband, because the wife never had control over the money. But by leaving it to the heirs, through the trust, the husband could make use of his lifetime gift exclusion, which would be $600,000 in 1987. Had it passed directly to his wife and then to his heirs, that portion of the money would have been subject to estate tax. This way it is not. Of course, if he had died before 1987, a lower lifetime gift and bequest allowance would be in effect.

Case III: An Estate of More Than $1,200,000

If the couple has more than $1,200,000 in property, say $2,000,000, they could combine some of the strategies above. One basic plan might be to split the estate. That way each could use the maximum tax-free exclusion — $600,000 in 1987. And the rates each would pay on the remaining $400,000 apiece would be somewhat lower than the rates one person would pay on leaving $800,000. Again, if the first spouse — let's say it's the wife — were to leave $1,000,000 to her heirs, in order to minimize estate taxes, she could still put it in trust, with the income from that amount going to her husband for life. The trust, once again, could be treated as a gift to the heirs under the lifetime gift exclusion.

Another alternative, says Mr. Hamm, is to take the part of the estate that would be taxable and leave it to the surviving spouse. Although the tax rate might be somewhat higher on the death of the husband, he would have been able to use all of the money until death. Had the wife left the money to someone else to minimize estate taxes, the tax might have been lower, but it would have been paid earlier.

Thus, $600,000 — not $1,000,000 — would go to the

heirs, either directly or in trust, on the death of the wife, to make use of the lifetime gift and bequest exclusion effective in 1987 and thereafter. And the remaining $1,400,000 would go to the husband. When the husband died, another $600,000 could be passed along tax-free (in 1987 and after), but the remaining $800,000 would be taxed.

The chart below shows the amount that may be transferred free of tax* during the coming years.

1981	$175,625
1982	$225,000
1983	$275,000
1984	$325,000
1985	$400,000
1986	$500,000
1987 and after	$600,000

* These limits do not hold if the beneficiary is married to the giver. Then, the tax-free amount that may be transferred is unlimited.

Because the estate tax is progressive, the tax on the $800,000 would be somewhat higher than if the wife had paid tax on $400,000 and the husband had paid tax on $400,000. But provided the husband does not die very soon after the wife, the fact that no tax had been paid until the death of the husband would probably more than make up for the higher tax rate. "Usually it takes only a few years of interest to make up for the tax rate differential," Mr. Hamm observes.

One asset that a couple might do away with entirely, with the new unlimited marital deduction, is insurance purchased to cover taxes on an estate to be left to a spouse. It is to take advantage of this change and others that tax specialists recommend that you review your whole estate program, including your will, in view of the new tax law. A will that was drafted to reap maximum benefits under the old tax code could leave you paying higher taxes now than you need to, unless you do some rearranging. "If you really want to take advantage of the new provisions, you have got to take action," cautions G. William Clapp, a partner at Deloitte Haskins & Sells.

Q: If I want to avoid estate taxes, should I leave my whole estate to my spouse?

A: Leaving your whole estate to your spouse would indeed make it a tax-free bequest, under the new law's unlimited tax-free marital transfer provision. But under the lifetime gift and bequest allowance, you could leave some money to others as well, without incurring any estate taxes. Furthermore, if you have a very large estate, the estate taxes on both your estate and on your spouse's may be less if you don't originally leave your whole estate to your spouse. While the new rules make it easier to escape taxes, it still requires some planning. This is one area where you would be well advised to consult with a professional estate planner if you have any significant amounts of property. Remember, the rapid inflation in housing prices of recent years has signficiantly increased the value of many people's assets.

Q: My spouse and I own our house jointly. Should we change this?

A: There may be an advantage in doing this, particularly if you think you know which of you is likely to die first. If the spouse who dies first was sole owner of the property, the house can still be given completely tax-free to the spouse, under the new unlimited marital transfer. Furthermore, the value of the house for tax purposes when it is inherited by the surviving spouse would be the market value at that time, which is likely to be higher than the price of the house when purchased. (This is known as "stepping up the basis.") Thus, when the surviving spouse decides to sell the house, the profit would probably be much smaller than it would have been, and the potential capital gains tax on the profit would also be lower.

If the spouse who does not own the house happens to die first, your estate tax bill will be no larger or smaller than it would have been if you held the house jointly. But you lose the advantage of raising the value of the house for capital gains tax purposes when it is sold. Had you simply continued to hold the house jointly, you would have hedged your bets, by being allowed to raise the tax value of the house for half of the house, but not for the other half. (The new law says that husband and wife are each to be considered half-owners of jointly held property nomatter who paid for it.)

Q: What do we have to do to change the ownership of the house?

A: You will need to make changes in the legal papers of ownership, and should probably seek the help of a lawyer in doing this.

Q: I have a terminal illness, and expect to die within six months. Is it worth while for my husband to try to transfer his share of our jointly owned house to me, so I can then will the whole house back to him?

A: If you die that soon after you have transferred ownership of the property, you can not increase the value of the property to minimize potential capital gains tax on the sale of your house. To take advantage of this technique, the transfer must take place at least one year prior to your death.

Q: Should we continue to own any of our assets as joint property, or would we be better off putting everything under one name or the other?

A: The only properties where it really pays to hold them in one name are properties that have appreciated greatly and thus where taxes on the profits could be sizable if the properties are sold. Therefore, it does not pay to shift the ownership of bank accounts or money market fund shares, which are not going to show capital gains. If, on the other hand, you happened to buy shares in International Business Machines or Xerox when those companies were founded, and they have soared in value, they would certainly be candidates for bequeathing to someone in order to minimize the capital gains tax. If you had shares that had increased greatly in value, you could give them to your spouse. When your spouse died, provided it was more than a year after your gift, and you inherited the shares, the capital gains tax when you sold the shares would be much lower.

Q: I am planning to buy some new life insurance. In the past, I have always made my spouse the owner of the policy. Should I continue to do this?

A: There is no longer any tax reason for doing this. However, you may want to consider putting the policy in trust for others to keep it out of both of your estates.

Q: My spouse and I each hold the life insurance policies on each other. Should we change this?

A: Under the new law, the estate tax consequences are the same whether you leave the policies in each other's names or put them under your own names.

10

Capital Gains

For investors, perhaps the best news in the new tax law is the reduction in the top rate on capital gains. Under the new law, the highest tax rate that you will have to pay for capital gains is 20 percent, a sizable reduction from the 28 percent ceiling that previously applied. As recently as 1978, the rate had been 49 percent.

The term capital gain simply refers to profits from the sale of an asset, as distinguished from dividends or interest payments. The investment could be stocks or bonds, silver or sapphires, artworks or antiques, a house or a hotel. As long as you hold that investment for more than a year, the gain is considered a long-term capital gain, and is eligible for preferential tax treatment. (When people refer to the capital gains tax, they almost always mean the tax on long-term capital gains.) Such profits have long enjoyed a preferential tax status, although the necessary holding period at one time was six months, rather than the year that it is now.

The latest reduction in the top tax rate on capital gains applies to assets sold after June 9, 1981, and should permit you to keep greater portions of any profits you make. But it could also have a profound effect on the marketplace, possibly altering the relative appeal of stocks and bonds and various other investments. Indeed, with the new law's more favorable treatment of capital gains, you would be well advised to review your investment strategies and financial plans. "It probably behooves many individuals to start taking greater risks in hopes of generating capital gains, rather than seeking income of other sorts," says George Ball, president of E. F. Hutton, the brokerage firm.

The capital gains rate applies not just to professional investors, but to anyone who sells an asset at a profit. If you sell your home, even that profit will be taxed at a capital gains rate unless you use the profit to buy another house within a certain period of time. (The new tax law also lengthens this period for rolling over the profits from your home without taxation.)

In fact, there really is no (long-term) capital gains tax rate, *per se*. Instead, there is a simple formula based on your income tax rate. The formula calls for you to exclude — or ignore — 60 percent of the capital gain. The remaining 40 percent is then taxed at the same rate you would pay on other income, such as dividends or interest payments. For this reason, the capital gains tax is really a graduated tax, just like the income tax.

Thus, under the previous tax law, if you were in the highest tax bracket — paying a marginal tax rate of 70 percent — you would have paid only 28 percent on long-term capital gains, that is, 70 percent tax on the 40 percent of the gain that is taxable. Let's say, for example, that you realized a $100,000 profit from selling some stock owned for more than a year. In figuring your tax, $60,000 would be excluded from taxable income altogether. After that, the 70 percent tax rate would be applied to the remaining $40,000, to produce a tax of $28,000. That $28,000 would represent a 28 percent tax on the $100,000 profit. Under the old tax law, if you were in the 35 percent tax bracket, you would have paid a capital gains tax of 14 percent (35 percent of 40 percent). If you had realized a profit of $100,000, you, too, would have excluded the first 60 percent of this gain, or $60,000. Then you would have applied your 35 percent tax rate to the remaining $40,000, for a tax of $14,000.

How the New Rate Works

The new tax law reduces the maximum rate to be paid on capital gains to 20 percent from 28 percent. It does this in a rather indirect fashion. It puts a new ceiling — of 50 percent — on the maximum tax rate for unearned income (that is, income from investments, rather than wage or salary income), significantly below the 70 percent top rate that had existed. With this sharp reduction in the maximum rate on unearned income, the effective top rate on capital gains falls to 20 percent from 28 percent, a clear boon to those in the highest tax brackets who would otherwise have been subject to capital gains taxes greater than 20 percent.

Even though the new ceiling rate on unearned income is not effective until January 1, 1982, Congress decided to lower the capital gains tax immediately. It did not want to have millions of investors postponing their investment moves just to pay lower taxes. So Congress voted for a retroactive measure providing that any profits realized after June 9, 1981, would not be subject to capital gains of more than 20 percent.

Lowering the top rate on capital gains benefits only those who have been in tax brackets above 50 percent. In the 50 percent bracket and below, the corresponding tax rates on capital gains will not change. But investors who were not in the top tax brackets will also find the capital gains rates they pay shrinking. Those reductions will be smaller and more gradual, resulting from the across-the-board cuts in the individual income tax rates that will be phased in over three years, starting October 1, 1981. Because the capital gains rate you pay is based on the tax rate you pay on ordinary income, the individual tax cuts mandated by the new law will automatically lower your capital gains tax as well.

While the new rule is relatively straightforward, Mr. Elinsky of Peat, Marwick cautions that there are some pitfalls. The first involves a situation where you have very little income other than sizable capital gains, which you take between June 10, 1981, and December 31, 1981. Because of the way in which the special transition rule is structured, you might find your whole capital gain subject to the 20 percent rate. Normally you would be able to apply lower, graduated rates to at least some of your capital gain.

Another quirk in the transition rule, Mr. Elinsky says, involves installment payments on assets sold on or before June

9. Any installments received in 1981 on assets sold on or before June 9 are *not* eligible for the new, lower capital gains treatments. But installments — from the same asset sale — that are received any time after December 31, 1981, *will* be eligible for the new, lower rates. "From a tax standpoint, installments received in 1982 instead of 1981 are better," Mr. Elinsky says. "The caveat, of course, is not to forget other considerations, such as whether you are comfortable that you will still receive your payment."

The Impact on Investments

While it is not difficult to figure out the impact of the new tax on a particular profit, assessing the new law's impact on various investment markets will be a good deal more challenging. In fact, several years after the fact, there is still controversy over the impact of the last reduction in the capital gains tax, in 1978.

Many proponents of a lower capital gains tax maintain that it spurs more investments in stocks, leading to higher stock prices. The lower capital gains tax is also widely believed to help the flow of money into venture capital. Indeed, it is investments such as these that are expected to benefit most from the latest cut in the capital gains tax.

Keep in mind, however, that at the same time that the top rate on capital gains is falling, the tax law is making other changes that will also significantly affect various forms of investment. The top tax rate on other forms of investment income, such as interest and dividends, is also being cut sharply. New incentives for savings — such as the tax-exempt savings certificates and the much broader program of tax-free retirement accounts — could also begin to shift flows of investment dollars. It may be some time before the markets come to a new equilibrium.

Notwithstanding these other changes, brokers are optimistic about the impact of the reduction in the top capital gains rate. "The new capital gains rates could have a favorable impact on the level of stock prices," says Mr. Ball, of E. F. Hutton. "The 80's could well be the era of the equity." But, he adds, other investments also stand to benefit from lower capital gains, including venture capital, discount bonds, timber lands, and real estate. In the case of timber land, for example, income from selling trees on property that has been held a year or more is treated as a capital gain, even if you still own the property.

Venture capital companies are usually those that are just starting out, and need large sums of money to support their growth until their own products begin to generate profits. For this reason, they are always searching for investment money, even though there are not enough profits yet to pay dividends. What they promise is the potential for big capital gains in the price of their shares of stock. A reduction in the capital gains rate allows investors to keep a larger portion of those profits, and therefore is expected to make such investments more appealing. "But," says Mr. Ball, who is also chairman of the tax policy and capital formation committee of the Securities Industry Association, "venture capital investments have become more attractive in recent years and have become very pricey. Most of them have become too expensive to buy into."

Discount bonds also are not new. A discount bond is simply a bond whose interest rate is set well below current interest rates, because it was first issued before interest rates had risen. If interest rates are hovering around 15 percent, for example, no one wants to buy a bond paying 8 percent interest. In order to sell it, its price must be cut sharply. It is now a discount bond. The best potential for appreciation comes if you are willing to hold the discount bond until it matures. Then, even if interest rates are still much higher than the rate on the bond, the issuer of the bond — usually a company or a government — will redeem it for its full price. If you had bought bonds with a face value of $10,000 for only $7,500, they would be redeemed for $10,000, giving you a capital gain of $2,500. With the new, lower capital gains tax, you would get to keep a higher proportion of the $2,500.

But while the reduction in the capital gains tax sheds a new light on some of these older investments, tax considerations should never be the overriding consideration in choosing an investment. Other factors, such as the potential for appreciation, should also be weighed. Investments that look good from a tax perspective, for example, should probably be bought very cautiously if they have already seen rapid price rises.

The new capital gains rates should also be kept in mind by property owners when it comes to deciding on how much depreciation to take on a tax return, says Mr. Powers of Deloitte Haskins & Sells. To the extent that you take accelerated depreciation, you may reduce the amount that qualifies for capital gains treatment when the property is sold. "So the investor may want to claim less accelerated depreciation to get more capital gains, depending on how long he intends to hold the property and on other circumstances," Mr. Powers says.

Selling a Home

The new law makes one other significant change in a special area of capital gains: the taxation of profits from the sale of a home. If it were not for these special provisions, the sale of your house would be subject to capital gains tax just like the sale of any other asset. But for a long time, housing has enjoyed a unique role in American society. As such, it has received special considerations under the tax code. The provisions, however, apply only to a house that is your principal residence, not to any other house that you may own.

Under the old tax law, you did not have to pay taxes on the sale of your home if you bought another within 18 months, either before or after the sale of your old home. However, the price of the new home had to equal or exceed the price you received for selling your old home. If your selling price exceeded the price of your new home, you would have had to pay capital gains tax on the difference, up to the actual amount of gain realized on the sale. The new law extends the 18-month period to 24 months if you sell your home after July 20, 1981, or within 18 months prior to that date.

Another facet of the old law allowed people who were 55 years or older and who sold their homes to exclude up to $100,000 in profits from taxes. The exclusion could only be taken once in a lifetime, and could be taken only if the house had been your principal residence for three of the five years preceding the sale.

The new law basically works just like the old law, except that it is more generous. People who are 55 or older may now exclude from taxes $125,000 in profits from the sale of a residence. It is still a one-time only exclusion, however. The new rule applies to any home sold after July 20, 1981.

These measures in themselves are likely to prove of little comfort to the housing market as long as interest rates remain high. But if you do sell your house — or any other asset — at a profit, the new rules could be very useful.

Q: What is a capital gain?

A: A capital gain is a profit from the sale of an asset, such as stocks or bonds, artworks, antiques, gems, gold, or real estate. If you hold the asset for more than 12 months, the gain is known as a long-term capital gain and will receive preferential tax treatment. If you do not hold it long enough to qualify for long-term capital gains, it will be deemed short-term capital gains and taxed like other unearned income, such as interest and dividends.

Q: Did the new tax law change the formula for calculating the capital gains rate? What is that formula?

A: The new law did not change the formula at all. The formula still allows you to exclude 60 percent of your capital gain from taxes. The remaining 40 percent is then taxed at the same rate as the rest of your income.

Q: What did the new tax law change?

A: The new law reduced the maximum capital gains rate you can pay to 20 percent from 28 percent.

Q: I have paid capital gains taxes and have never had to pay the maximum rate. Will there be reductions below the maximum rate too?

A: There will be no other formal reductions in the capital gains rate. But since the rate on capital gains is based on your income tax rate, the effective rate you pay will fall slightly as your income tax rate is reduced over the three years beginning October 1, 1981.

Q: Did the new law change the holding period for long-term capital gains?

A: No. You still have to hold an asset for more than one year to qualify for tax treatment of the profits as long-term capital gains.

Q: Will any of the capital gains I realized in 1981 be eligible for the lower capital gains rate?

A: Yes. Capital gains from any assets sold after June 9, 1981, will be eligible for the more favorable capital gains treatment under the new law. Although the new tax structure did not become law until August, Congress made the capital gains provisions retroactive, to prevent people from postponing their sales of assets.

Q: I sold a property in 1980, but am being paid in five annual installments. Will any of the installments qualify under the new capital gains rates?

A: Installments received in 1981 would not qualify for the more favorable capital gains treatment, but installments received in 1982 and thereafter would.

Q: With the more favorable capital gains treatment, should I buy stocks?

A: If you are paying the maximum capital gains rate, any profits you make by buying and selling stocks would indeed be taxed less heavily under the new law. But whether you make any profits depends in large part on what happens to the stock market, and particularly to the stocks you pick. Some investment advisers think the lower capital gains tax will indeed spur new interest in the stock market, helping to send the market up. But it is not a foregone conclusion. Other factors, such as interest rates, also affect the market, as they quite clearly did in the weeks following the passage of the new tax law, when the stock market dropped sharply.

Q: I plan to retire in 1982. I have been in my company pension plan for 16 years. I was thinking of taking my pension benefits in one lump sum. Can I use the capital gains rate when figuring the tax on this money?

A: Since you were in the pension plan before 1974, you can choose to apply the capital gains tax rate to some of the money you receive from your pension plan, but not all of it. The capital gains tax may be used only for the portion of your pension that applies to your years of service before 1974. Since roughly half of your pension comes from pre-1974 service, you can apply the capital gains treatment to half of what you receive. Before you do this, however, calculate your taxes both under the capital gains treatment and under the 10-year-averaging formula that now applies to pension payments. Then choose the one that minimizes your taxes.

Q: We are planning to sell our house. What kind of taxes do we have to pay?

A: If the house is your principal residence, you do not have to pay any tax on the profits from its sale if — within two years either before or after the sale — you invest the money in a house that will be your new principal residence and that costs as much or more as the one you sold. Also, if you are 55 or older, you can exclude $125,000 of your profits on the sale of your home from tax, even if you do not buy a new home. This exclusion may only be used once in your lifetime, however, and must be applied to a house that has been your principal residence for at least three of the five years preceding the sale.

Q: We recently sold our home for $150,000. The following week, we bought a new home for $125,000. Will we have to pay any taxes?

A: That depends on whether you made any profit from selling your house. If you had bought it for $150,000 and sold it for $150,000, there would be no profit to tax. Then it would not matter whether you bought a new house at all. Since you did buy a new house, it does not matter what the cost was. On the other hand, if you bought your house for $100,000 and then sold it for $150,000, at a $50,000 profit, you will be subject to taxes on $25,000 of the profit since your new house cost $25,000 less than you sold your old house for.

Q: We have a summer home that we are planning to sell. How will that be taxed? Does it matter whether or not we have rented the house to other people?

A: Since the summer home is not your principal residence, your profits will be taxed. If you used the house entirely for yourselves, and did not rent it out or depreciate it, then all of your profits will be taxed as capital gains — long-term capital gains if you have held the house for more than a year.

The main difference is that if you have rented the house to others and depreciated the house, the calculations for figuring your profits will be somewhat different. Let's say you bought the house for $40,000 and sold it for $100,000. If you never took any depreciation, your profit would be $60,000.

But if you depreciated the house by $10,000, then you would have to pay taxes on $70,000. Of that, $60,000 will still be taxed at a capital gains rate. The tax rate on the $10,000 that you depreciated will depend on what kind of depreciation you took. If it was straight-line depreciation, all of the depreciation would also be taxed at the capital gains rate. But if you used accelerated depreciation, the amount of depreciation you were able to take over and above what you would have gotten under straight-line depreciation would be subject to ordinary income tax rates.

Q: I am 60 years old and sold my house at a profit of $150,000 in March 1981. I am not planning to buy another house. How much can I exclude from taxes?

A: Since you sold your home before July 21, 1981, you are eligible only for the old exclusion of $100,000, rather than the new exclusion of $125,000. Therefore, $50,000 of your profit will be taxable.

11

Working Abroad

If there were ever a time to live and work abroad, it is now — at least according to tax experts. On January 1, 1982, the new tax law ushers in some of the most favorable provisions for taxing expatriates in 20 years.

How these changes will affect you if you are already working overseas depends largely on your individual circumstances. Whether your employer already helps with your tax payments, and what the taxes are in the country in which you work, will be important factors in determining how much personal benefit you derive from the new law. "As a general rule, the new law could offer a significant reduction in United States taxes for many Americans overseas," says Robert H. Castles, director of expatriate services at Arthur Young, the accounting firm.

If your employer already pays for the higher tax costs you face by working abroad, you will probably see little change under the new law. It has become the norm among most major companies with employees abroad to pay not only the extra costs of living abroad — such as housing and schooling and foreign tax — but also the tax on the extra income these sums represent. In these cases, the companies will benefit. "From our employees' point of view, this bill is neither here nor there," says George J. Clark, executive vice president at Citibank. "We have picked up the tax burden, and will also pick up the benefit."

By lowering the expense of supporting employees abroad,

however, the new law is expected to lead to a spurt in overseas job opportunities for Americans, in a dramatic reversal of the shrinkage of the past few years. In a survey of 306 United States companies, Organization Resources Counselors, an economic research firm, found that the number of American expatriates fell by 39 percent in 1980, to 22,580; in 1979, there had been 37,000. This shrinkage occurred as the number of expatriates from other countries was doubling.

Although the weakness of the dollar at that time was believed to have contributed to the decline, it was widely agreed within the corporate community that United States tax policy had been the critical factor. American corporations were major proponents of the new tax rules for expatriates, which, they argued, would help increase American exports and therefore boost the American economy. They contended that having Americans in positions overseas would result in those executives ordering more American equipment. Whether that occurs remains to be seen. What is clear is that many companies plan to send more Americans to staff their overseas offices.

Who Will Benefit From the Exclusions

Beginning in 1982, you will be allowed to exclude from your taxable income up to $75,000 of the income you earn abroad. That exclusion will rise by $5,000 a year, until it reaches $95,000 in 1986. You may also be able to exclude some of your foreign housing costs from taxable income, although fewer people are likely to be able to take this exclusion than the income exclusion.

Even if your company picks up the tab for extra tax incurred in working abroad, you should look at the new tax rules. For while the new provisions deal directly with the income you earn abroad, they will indirectly affect your other income as well. For example, if you work overseas, you are likely to find your investment income taxed at lower rates under the new law. On the other hand, you may also find that you are barred from putting money into tax-free Individual Retirement Accounts or from taking the new marriage deduction. You must have taxable income from earnings to be eligible for tax-free retirement accounts. And the new law specifically bars those who take a foreign income exclusion from claiming the marriage penalty relief.

The new provisions should substantially reduce the high cost of supporting an American abroad. One tax executive at a major New York corporation estimated that the cost of supporting an American with a salary of $30,000 a year in a foreign country typically has been about $120,000, including salary, housing, education, home leave, and tax. Tax would amount to about $45,000 of that total, he said. Under the new law, that $45,000 would be cut sharply. It is cuts such as these that are expected to make sending Americans abroad attractive again.

"We anticipate that there will be a real increase in the number of United States workers abroad," says Miles Bresee, manager of taxes at the Bechtel Group, a San Francisco-based engineering and construction company with a sizable overseas business, particularly in the Middle East. He says that not only will the company be able to afford more American workers on its current projects, but with the lower costs, Bechtel could be more competitive and would probably win more projects overseas. Other companies also plan to send more Americans abroad. Joseph F. Alibrandi, president of the Whittaker Corporation of Los Angeles, for example, has said that he plans to increase substantially the proportion of Americans in his company's foreign work force under the more favorable tax provisions. Currently, Americans constitute only 10 to 15 percent of the 3,000 people Whittaker uses abroad in managing hospitals. The company hopes to raise that figure to approximately 50 percent. Citibank, too, expects to send more Americans abroad. "Before, if we had a Frenchman and an American who were equal in every way, we had to choose the Frenchman for tax reasons," Mr. Clark says. "Now that bias is removed. Over time, we will have more Americans working abroad than we would have otherwise."

But at the Chase Manhattan Bank, Walter Lamp, a vice president in the tax department, cautions, "Taxes are only one of our costs of doing business. We could now have room to put more people overseas, or we could make other adjustments, such as becoming more competitive."

American companies are not the only ones viewing American workers with new interest. Gilbert Dwyer, a partner at Ward Howell International, an executive recruiting firm, who specializes in recruiting for positions in the Middle East, says that foreign employers — both business and government — are also looking at the American labor market from a new perspective. Shortly after the new tax law was signed, one of his Saudi Arabian clients expressed possible interest in hiring more Americans.

Who Qualifies

For individuals who are working abroad or considering the possibility, the new rules, which permit broad exclusions of income and housing costs from American taxes, are in many ways easier to use than the provisions they are replacing. The old law, effective since 1978, determined expatriate taxes by considering a long and complex list of variables, including country of residence, cost of living, housing and schooling expenses, and costs incurred in home leave.

The new law, like the old, does call for an individual to meet certain qualifications to be eligible for the new foreign income exclusions, but the rules have been somewhat loosened. Under the new law, an individual must meet one of the following two tests.

RESIDENCE: The first condition calls for residence in a foreign country for one full taxable year — a test that also existed under the old law. (A person who moves abroad in the middle of a calendar year may — with permission — extend his tax filing for the year until the residence test is met. The foreign income rules, however, would apply only to the portion of the year spent abroad.)

PHYSICAL PRESENCE: The second test calls for being physically present in a country for 11 months out of any 12-month period. The test in the old law required physical presence in a foreign country for 17 months in any 18-month period.

People who meet either of these requirements may choose to protect some of their foreign income from American tax. Tax advisers caution, however, that, while such exclusions are usually helpful, they are not best for everyone.

The Income Exclusion

In 1982, you may exclude up to $75,000 of the income you earned abroad from your taxable income. That figure will rise by $5,000 a year, until it reaches $95,000 in 1986; it will remain at that level unless Congress makes further changes. Only income received as compensation in a foreign assignment is eligible for exclusion from your American taxable income. Generally, if you work for the American government (and this includes the military), you may not take the exclusion.

Other kinds of income received abroad, such as payments from a pension or an annuity or interest and dividend income, do not qualify for the exclusion either. However, because of the exclusion, you will probably find your other income, such as investment income, being taxed at lower tax brackets. Let's say, for example, that you earned a $50,000 salary abroad in 1982 and had an additional $10,000 in interest on bank accounts in the United States. Under the new law, only the $50,000 in earned income could be excluded from your taxable income. The other $10,000 would be taxable in the United States. But it would be taxed as if it were your only taxable income — and thus at a tax rate much lower than if you were also paying U.S. taxes on the other $50,000 as well.

Housing Costs

The most confusing of the new provisions for expatriates is the section dealing with housing. There is a possible exclusion for housing expenses, but few people will be eligible to take it. That is because your housing exclusion combined with your income exclusion may not exceed your foreign earned income. This means that if your foreign earnings did not exceed the maximum possible income exclusion — $75,000 in 1982 — you generally would not be eligible for any additional exclusion for your housing costs abroad. An exception: individuals who do not use the income exclusion, but who do elect to take the housing exclusion.

Even if you are eligible for the housing exclusion, there would be a minimum level of expenses that you could not exclude. Congress set that level equal to 16 percent of the salary of a United States Government employee at the GS-14 Step 1 level. In 1981, that 16 percent came to $6,059, a figure that will rise as Government salaries increase. Thus, if you had housing costs of $5,000 in 1982, and you otherwise qualified for the housing provision, you would not be able to exclude or deduct your housing expense because it did not exceed $6,059. If you had housing costs of $10,000 in 1982, however, and qualified for the exclusion or deduction, you would be allowed to exclude or deduct $3,941 — the difference between $10,000 and $6,059.

Consider the case of an expatriate with $50,000 in foreign income in 1982 and $10,000 in housing costs. That person could exclude all $50,000 from taxable income. But any exclusion that person tried to take for housing would immediately push the total exclusions over the person's foreign income, the law's limit.

This is in contrast to the individual who earned $100,000 overseas in 1982. Since this person could exclude only $75,000 of salary from taxable income, there would be room to take a housing exclusion of up to $25,000 as well. If the person had $20,000 in housing costs, he would first have to subtract the $6,059 base. Then he could exclude $13,941 from American taxes, as well as his $75,000 income exclusion, because the total exclusions of $88,941 would not exceed his income of $100,000.

Foreign Tax Payments

Despite the more favorable American tax policy, if you are working in a country where you have to pay tax to the host government, you will still be liable for that foreign tax. Furthermore, many expatriates will find they are not able to count that foreign tax as a credit against their American tax. In some situations, however, it will be possible.

Among those who will find they can not take any credit for foreign tax will be everyone who excludes all of his earned income from American tax (mostly those whose foreign income does not exceed the maximum exclusion — $75,000 in 1982). That is because the American Government has already excused these people from paying tax on their foreign earned income; any further credit could amount to a subsidy of the foreign tax. "The idea is to eliminate double taxation, not to create double benefits," says John R. Raedel, a partner at Peat, Marwick, Mitchell. "In cases where a person is faced with foreign taxes higher than his American tax liability would be, the expatriate is really in no better position with the new tax law than he was with the old."

But, if your foreign income is too big to exclude from American tax entirely (as it might be in Japan or in Scandinavian countries), you will be allowed to credit some, but not all, of any foreign tax you pay against your American tax bill.

Consider the case of an individual who earns $100,000 abroad in 1982, and has no other income. In calculating his American tax bill, he could exclude $75,000 from taxable income. But he would still be required to pay American tax on $25,000. Because he is paying American tax on $25,000, or one-quarter of his income, and paying foreign tax on all $100,000 of his income, he would effectively be taxed twice on that $25,000. To get around that, the new tax law would allow him to take a credit against his American tax for some — but not all — of his foreign tax bill. How that credit will work will be spelled out in regulations. It is expected that it will be handled on some kind of proportionate basis. In this example, since the expatriate is being taxed twice on one-quarter of his income, he would probably be allowed to take a credit against his American taxes for one-quarter of his foreign tax bill. Thus, if he were faced with a $16,000 tax bill from his foreign host country, he might be allowed to take a $4,000 credit on his American tax bill. The credit may not exceed the American tax owed on the income earned abroad. In the case above, for example, if the expatriate owed $4,500 in American taxes on his $25,000 of foreign income, he could use the $4,000 as a credit against it.

There is, however, a limit to the foreign tax credit, a limit that will affect expatriates in countries with tax rates higher than those in the United States. If the foreign tax bill had been higher — say $40,000 instead of $16,000 — and he tried to take a $10,000 credit (one quarter of the foreign tax bill) against his $4,500 in American taxes, he could not take it all in one year; he would be limited to $4,500. But, the remaining $5,500 could be carried back two years and forward five years to be used as a credit, if possible, in those years.

The amount of foreign earned income that may be excluded from U.S. taxes:

Year	$
1982	$75,000
1983	$80,000
1984	$85,000
1985	$90,000
1986 and after	$95,000

A final reminder: Foreign taxes may be credited only against American taxes owed on foreign income, not against American taxes on income from other sources.

Because of these rules on foreign taxes, it may sometimes pay for expatriates not to use the exclusions that are available. Tax experts say some Americans abroad may be better off utilizing all of their foreign tax credits against their American taxes and carrying the credits backward and forward. Once employees use the exclusions, if they then opt out, they may not use the exclusions again for five years without special permission from the Treasury Department. "The decision not to elect the exclusions is probably atypical, but not so rare that you should automatically ignore it," Mr. Raedel said.

And, Mr. Castles added, "If you have to transfer from country to country, particularly countries with different tax structures, you are going to find it more difficult to plan the best tax results. Under the new law, the emphasis for expatriates has changed from dual country tax planning to foreign country tax planning. Now it will pay for expatriates to concentrate on reducing their foreign taxes."

Q: How long do I have to be overseas to qualify for the deductions?

A: You must either live abroad for an uninterrupted period of at least one taxable year, or you must be present in a foreign country (or countries) for at least 330 days during a 12-month period. If you travel back and forth between the foreign country and the United States frequently, you may find it easier to qualify under the foreign residence test where your days of physical presence are not actually counted. In that case, you must also be subject to the foreign country's tax laws to qualify for the special treatment in the United States.

Q: What happens if I go overseas in the middle of a tax year?

A: When you move abroad, but do not yet qualify for the foreign exclusion because you have not been abroad long enough, you can request an extension of your tax filing date until you meet the qualification. Otherwise, you can file your tax return as usual and amend it later.

Q: What happens if I go to a foreign country and then travel to a third country for a while — or come back to the United States for vacation. Does that affect my ability to qualify for the deductions?

A: You must still meet the requirements of one of the two specified tests. Such travel affects your physical presence, but not your proof of residence.

Q: If I have to pay foreign taxes, can I deduct them from my American taxes?

A: You can take a tax credit in the United States for foreign tax payments only if you have foreign earned income that you have not already claimed an exclusion for on your American tax return. Thus if you had $50,000 of foreign earned income and you took an exclusion for all $50,000, you could take no tax credits for foreign tax payments. But if you had $100,000 of foreign earned income and you took an exclusion for $75,000 of that, you would be able to claim a credit for a portion of the taxes you paid abroad. There are limits on how much of a credit you could claim.

Q: What happens if I have income from investments in the United States while I am abroad? How is that treated?

A: This income generally could not be excluded from your taxable income. But if all of your foreign income were excluded from American taxes, your investment income would be taxed as if it were the only income you had, and thus at relatively low rates. If it were only a few thousand dollars, it might be covered entirely by your personal exemptions and your standard deduction, leaving you with no taxable income in the United States.

Q: If I am allowed special deductions for housing, education, cost of living and home leave travel under the old tax law, will I still be allowed them under the new law?

A: No. The item-by-item deductions in the old law will no longer hold, starting in 1982. They will be replaced by the more general exclusions for income and housing.

Q: Do I *have* to take the new income exclusion if I work abroad?

A: No, it is entirely elective. In some cases, you may even be better off not taking it. Once you elect the exclusion, if you revoke it without permission from the Internal Revenue Service, you may not elect it again for five years without specific permission. This is to prevent people from taking unfair advantage of the exclusion, though it could cause problems for people who are legitimately moved around for job-related reasons.

Q: When should I not take the exclusion?

A: This must be determined on a case-by-case basis. You might consider not taking the exclusion if you are in a country with taxes higher than the United States or if you are likely to move frequently, particularly from one foreign country to another. In such cases, you probably would benefit from consulting a specialist familiar with both U.S. and foreign taxes.

Q: If I receive some final paychecks after I return from a foreign assignment, can those be excluded from American income tax?

A: Yes, provided you have met all of the other tests and the payments were for services overseas. They must, however, be received within one tax year following your last year of service abroad.

Q: If I qualify for the housing exclusion, is there any limit on the amount I may exclude?

A: Yes, there are several limitations. First, the housing exclusion combined with the income exclusion (if used) may not exceed your total income earned abroad. Second, the law requires that housing expenses be reasonable. There appears to be quite a bit of latitude in defining what is reasonable.

Q: Government employees generally are not eligible for these new expatriate provisions, because they are generally exempt from foreign taxes. If the spouse of a Government employee has a job overseas, may the spouse make use of the foreign earned income exclusion?

A: If the Government employee's spouse has a non-Government job, the foreign earned income exclusion may be used to cover that one income.

Q: If I have to leave a foreign assignment because war breaks out in the country before I qualify for the tax exclusions, can I qualify anyway?

A: Maybe. The new tax law, like the old, provides that people can take the exclusions without meeting the usual requirements if they were living in a foreign country and were required to leave because of civil unrest or war, and can prove that they would have qualified for the exclusions if they had not been required to leave. However, like anyone who was not in a foreign country for a whole year, they will have to pro-rate the exclusion to cover only the time they were there.

12

Incentive Stock Options for Employees

Employees who receive stock options from their companies will find the new tax code treats these options quite handsomely. Congress was not trying to reward corporate executives, although that is an outgrowth of the new law. Its aim, rather, was to help small, start-up companies attract and hold people, because these companies are believed to be an important factor in technological research and innovation. Since they are so new, however, these small companies often can not pay salaries that are competitive with larger companies. Instead, many give stock options. Under the new law, these options will be worth more to the employees, making them a better recruiting tool for companies.

"There are some real potential payoffs there for employees who are willing to gamble," says David N. Swinford, a principal at Sibson & Company, a Princeton-based management consulting firm specializing in employee compensation. He notes that the greater attractiveness of options under the new law could also prompt other, larger companies to use them more actively as well.

The new attraction of the employee stock option stems from two changes in the tax law. One change, which shifts the tax on options to a capital gains rate from the tax rate on wages, effectively slashes the maximum tax rate on options from 50 percent to 20 percent. The other change allows taxes on options to be deferred until the stock is sold. Under the old law, if you bought stock through an option, you had to pay taxes when you exercised your option and purchased stock, instead of waiting until you sold the stock. (Like most tax payments, these were made when you filed your annual tax return.) If the stock went down before you sold it, you would effectively have paid taxes on profits you never got.

A stock option is simply an agreement that gives the holder the right to purchase a number of shares of stock at a set price for some period of months or years. If the market price rises, the option holder can still buy the stock at the previously agreed price, making a sure profit. If the stock doesn't rise, the option holder can ignore the option, without having money tied up in the stock.

For example, you might have an option to buy stock in XYZ Corp. at $25 a share. When the price in the stock market is at or below $25, the option does not provide you with a bargain; you could buy the stock in the open market at or below the option price. But if the stock moves to $35 a share in the market, and you've still got an option allowing you to buy the stock at $25, your option is worth $10 a share. At that point it may make sense to exercise your option to buy the stock at $25 a share, since you can turn around and sell it at $35 a share.

The flexibility of being able to hold an option without actually buying the stock until it suits you can be quite valuable. In fact, thousands of stock options are bought and sold everyday, just as stock and bonds are, on the Chicago Board Options Exchange, the American Stock Exchange and other exchanges around the country. The exchange-traded options are standardized, and can be traded by anyone.

But companies also use stock options as incentives and rewards for employees. Traditionally, such options have been given to the very highest executives, people in a position to affect the value of a company's stock. The theory is that options give the executives an extra incentive to do their jobs well and thus to lift the price of the companies' stock, because that would probably cause their options to gain in value, too. These options are not traded on any exchange, and, in fact, generally do not change hands at all. But the new tax rules apply only to these corporate incentive options.

Of course, the real test of a successful option depends on how much the stock itself rises, rather than on the taxes paid or not paid. But once there are gains, tax treatment is important in determining how much of a gain the employee keeps. And the new law is a big improvement over the existing law, which requires gains from options to be treated as earned income and taxed at rates as high as 50 percent.

Stock options have long received some form of preferential treatment. The stock options rule phased out between 1976 and May 1981, for example, was similar to the new rule in that it allowed holders of "qualified" options to pay taxes on their gains from those options only after they had sold their stock. But to qualify, the stock had to be held for three years, a period many executives felt was uncomfortably long.

After May 1981 — and before the new tax law was passed — an employee exercising an option had to pay taxes on the gain from the option at the time of exercise, treating that gain just like any other type of wage or salary income. Thus, if you had an option to buy stock at $30 a share, and actually bought stock when the price rose to $50 in the stock market, you would have been taxed on income of $20 a share, even if you planned to hold the stock for months or years. (The need to pay taxes, as well as to pay for the stock, often left employees scraping for funds, which may have come out of their own savings or from a loan from a bank or from their companies.) Employees often do not sell their shares immediately upon purchase, either because they are not allowed to for various reasons, or because they hope to qualify for long-term capital gains treatment, or because they wish to hold the shares for further appreciation.

If, in the example above, after the stock rose another $10 a share in the marketplace, to $60, you decided to sell your shares, you would then pay capital gains tax on the additional $10 profit: at the long-term capital gains rate if the shares themselves had been held for more than a year, and at the short-term rate if you had held them for a year or less. On the other hand, if, after you had exercised your option, the stock plummeted to $15 from $50, you could then take a capital loss of $35.

The new law basically applies to new options, granted after the law was passed, as long as they meet certain qualifications. But it also will make some options issued earlier eligible for this more favorable tax treatment, provided they meet the same requirements. Where existing option plans do not meet these standards, companies may choose to try to make them conform, if they wish. "Executives with outstanding options may have a nice windfall, assuming their companies are willing to provide them," comments George R. Ince, a manager in the tax department at Ernst & Whinney.

There will be some limitations on any windfalls, however. To qualify, the options must have been given no earlier than 1976. And an executive may apply the new laws to existing options that totaled no more than $50,000 a year, based on the price when granted, and no more than $200,000 for all past years.

Even employees who exercised options in early 1981 may be able to apply the new tax treatment to their options, provided those options also meet the same requirements. But if they do not meet the requirements exactly, the company can not change the option agreement to conform, as it can with the outstanding, unexercised options. Tax experts say that there may be some options exercised in early 1981 that might qualify under this rule, but they expect the number to be relatively small.

Despite the generally favorable treatment of stock options in the new law, there are some drawbacks as well. One is that it requires all options to be exercised in the order in which they were granted. This means, for example, that you would have to exercise options granted in 1983 before you could exercise options given in 1984 or 1985. The problem with this is that depending on how the company's stock has performed, you might find yourself backed into buying more expensive stock, while you had options outstanding to buy less expensive stock.

For example, let's say XYZ Corp.'s stock is at $40 a share in 1983, when it gives you options to buy 1,000 shares of the stock at $40 a share. A year later, the stock falls to $30 a share, and you are given options to buy the stock at $30. A couple of years later, with the stock back up at $40, you decide to exercise the $30 options, which are showing a $10 a share profit. To do so, you would have to exercise the $40 options first if you still wanted to retain the new, more favored tax treatment. While you may not lose any money in doing so, you would have to raise more money to buy the additional shares that you do not really want. Of course, if your stock does nothing but climb upward, this is not a problem.

How the New Provisions Work

Under the new law, if you exercise options that meet certain criteria — which the Act then labels Incentive Stock Options, or I.S.O.'s — you will not be required to pay any taxes in connection with those options until you actually sell your stock. Then, any profit from the sale will be taxed at long-term capital gains rates, provided two additional conditions are met:

First, the stock must be held at least two years beyond the original granting of the option, and for at least one year beyond the date on which the option is exercised and the stock purchased. Second, you must stay at the company that granted the option until at least three months before the option is exercised. That means that if you retire or leave a company, you should plan to exercise your options within three months of departure. If you do not remain with the company long enough, you forfeit the favored tax status on your options, and will have to pay ordinary income tax on the gains when you exercise your options.

ELIGIBILITY REQUIREMENTS: To be eligible for such favorable tax treatment, however, options must meet certain requirements spelled out in the new tax act.

● The option plan must be approved by shareholders within 12 months of its adoption. Options must then be granted within 10 years from the date the plan was adopted, or from the date that it was approved, whichever came first.

● The plan must specify the number of shares to be issued and the employees eligible for the options.

● The option is nontransferable except at the death of the holder.

• Employees must exercise their options within ten years of their being granted, or five years if the employee owns more than 10 percent of the company.

• Companies must try to insure that the exercise price of the option is at least equal to the price of the company's shares when the option is granted. To protect against potential abuse, if you own more than 10 percent of a company, the option price must be at least 10 percent higher than the market price at the date the option is issued.

• Options must be exercised in the order granted.

Beginning in 1981, a company may grant up to $100,000 of incentive stock options to an employee in any one year. But if this full grant is not used in any one year, an employee may carry over half of the unused portion for up to three years, making it possible for an employee to be granted options valued at $250,000 in one year. Of course, a company, if it wishes, may grant options worth even more. But anything over these prescribed limits would not be eligible for the more favored tax provisions.

Existing options, to be eligible for the new, more favorable tax treatment, must meet these same standards. If an existing option plan does not conform completely, a company has a year to make it eligible, if it cares to. Tax specialists say that employees who have exercised options in 1981 will be eligible for the preferential tax treatment if their options also conform. "If an executive has already exercised an option, the company can't amend the option agreement to make it conform," says Mr. Ince, at Ernst & Whinney. "But if the option has not yet been exercised, a company has a year to qualify the plan if it wishes." He and others recommend that companies wishing to give their employees options valued at greater than $100,000 each year set up separate option plans, one that would meet the requirements to qualify it for the special tax treatment (including the $100,000 limit), and one that would not.

While nonqualifying options would not be quite as attractive from a tax perspective as the special Incentive Stock Options, they could still be quite profitable for the employee. The new law makes even these options more lucrative, because of the reduction in the maximum capital gains tax rate to 20 percent from 28 percent. All you have to do to qualify for the capital gains rate is to hold the stock at least a year.

For top corporate executives who are granted options worth more than $100,000 each year, the new law will not make a significant difference. But for other executives, particularly middle managers and technical and professional people whose compensation is not quite as grand, the new law could make a significant difference.

Q: The new tax law says that existing options, as well as ones issued after the new law was passed, may be eligible for more favorable treatment. I still have options from 1975. Could they qualify under the new tax rules?

A: No. The new tax law is indeed retroactive: It allows some existing options to qualify for special tax treatment, if they meet all of the requirements spelled out in the new law for Incentive Stock Options. But to qualify, they must have been granted on or after January 1, 1976.

Q: My company is willing to give me options for stock at a price that is even less than the price in the market today. Isn't there a requirement that the price can not be below the market price?

A: There is nothing to stop your company from giving you options to buy shares below the market price. Just recognize that they will not qualify for the favored tax treatment spelled out in the new law. There may be some cases where the low option price would be more desirable than the special tax treatment. But, in general, the tax provisions are so much more favorable that you would probably be better off making sure the options did qualify under the new law. If there were other reasons why the options would not qualify, however, then by all means go for the lower price as well.

Q: My company only gives stock options to a few top executives. But when it does, the options usually are for $200,000 or $300,000 of stock. The new law says that any option for more than $100,000 of stock will not qualify. What should I do?

A: Try to get your company to spread the options out so that no option represents more than $100,000 in any one year. Or ask the company to give you two options, one for $100,000 of stock that will qualify for the special tax treatment and one for any shares over and above $100,000 that would not qualify. Tax experts believe that so long as the two sets of options are kept separate, it would be possible to take full advantage of the new tax provisions while not limiting the options you receive.

Q: May I use previously acquired stock in the company to pay for additional options I am granted?
A: Yes.

Q: What happens if I would have otherwise qualified for the incentive stock option provisions but I do not hold the stock until a date two years after the option is granted, as required by law?
A: Your shares no longer qualify for the special tax provisions. According to Peat, Marwick, Mitchell, you would calculate the taxes you would pay in two steps. First, you would pay ordinary income tax on the lesser of two amounts, your profit on the sale of the stock, or the difference between the price you paid for your shares and the value of the stock when you exercised your option. Then, any additional gain would be taxed at the capital gains rate — long-term capital gains if you had held the stock for at least a year, and short-term capital gains if you had held the stock for a shorter period.
Let's say you had an option to buy your company's stock at $20 a share. When the price of the stock rose to $50, you exercised your option, buying the stock at $20. Then you sold your stock when it reached $60, even though you had not met the holding-period requirements. Even though you had a profit of $40 a share (the difference between the price you sold at and the price you bought at), you could elect to pay ordinary income tax on only $30 a share (the difference between the price when you exercised the option and the price you bought the stock at). The remaining $10 would be subject to capital gains tax. If you had held them for a year or longer, that would qualify for long-term capital gains treatment, with a maximum rate of 20 percent. If the price at which you sold your shares was $45 a share, rather than $60, your profit would be only $25 a share. In this case, the route to the lowest tax would simply be to pay ordinary income tax on the $25 a share profit, rather than to use the alternate, two-step computation.

Q: What happens if I sell the stock I acquired through a stock option less than a year after I exercised the option?
A: Once again, your option would no longer qualify for the

special tax treatment. You would be taxed in the same fashion as in the example above. The only difference would be that if any portion of your profit were treated as a capital gain, it definitely would not qualify as a long-term capital gain.

Q: If the stock price in my company jumps around, so that my later stock options are at lower prices than my earlier ones, do I still have to exercise them in chronological order?

A: No. But if you exercise later options first, the more favorable tax treatment does not apply. Depending on the relative prices and your tax situation, it may sometimes make sense to give up the special tax treatment. You should work through the arithmetic carefully before making such a decision.

Q: My company has decided to qualify some of its past options, by changing them to meet all the new requirements. I have already exercised some of these options. Will those options be eligible for the new tax treatment?

A: Probably not. Options already exercised that did not exactly meet the qualifications when exercised will be subject to the old tax provisions, not the new ones. But if you have any of those options that you have not yet exercised, they would be eligible for the more favorable tax treatment, even though they were granted before the new law was passed.

13
Tax Shelters

On January 1, 1981, the maximum income tax rate for individuals tumbles from 70 percent to 50 percent. That reduction in the top rate will slice hundreds of millions of dollars from the tax bills of upper-income Americans. At the same time, it could cut deeply into the traditional market for tax shelters: people in tax brackets greater than 50 percent.

There are dozens of kinds of tax shelters, ranging from oil drilling and real estate to movie companies and solar energy projects. What they all have in common is that they are investments that help reduce your taxes, at least for a few years. Generally they do this by generating tax losses. Since they are set up as partnerships rather than corporations, you are allowed to take the losses directly on your tax return. Each $1 of loss that you write off reduces your taxable income by $1. In a 70 percent tax bracket, that would save you 70 cents in tax; in a 50 percent tax bracket, it would save you 50 cents. There is nothing to prevent people in 30 percent tax brackets from investing in tax shelters, and saving 30 cents, but generally the shelters will not be worth as much to someone in a lower tax bracket as they are to someone in a higher tax bracket.

There are limits to the losses you are allowed to write off. Except in a few specific kinds of tax shelters, you may write off no more than the amount you have at risk in the project. Let's take the case of a $4 million project that raised $1 million from you and other investors, and then borrowed another $3 million in financing. Typically, you and other investors would be allowed to write off losses of up to $1 million. If, however, you and the other investors were personally liable for the $3 million in financing, you would be at risk for this amount as well, and you would be allowed to write off up to $4 million in losses. There are a few exceptions, such as subsidized housing, where you would be allowed to write off losses up to the value of the debt plus your equity, even though you are not liable for the debt. In this kind of shelter, depending on your tax bracket, you could defer paying $2 or $3 in taxes for every $1 you invested, even if the project never showed any profit. Where the tax benefits are so generous, you may be willing to invest in projects with very high risks that you would otherwise not consider.

On the other hand, a tax shelter does not necessarily have to lose money forever. Some tax shelters, those with real economic value, may eventually start to show profits. Then you gain not only from the tax deductions, but also from the profits. When the profits start to roll in, it is time to look for another investment to shelter those profits.

The fact that there will no longer be investors in tax brackets above 50 percent will definitely put a crimp in the tax shelter industry. Most tax specialists, however, do not expect the industry to be put out of business. "Fifty percent is still a high tax burden, especially after you start adding state and local taxes," observes Daniel Kruger, a tax partner at Peat, Marwick, Mitchell. He predicts that there would be many taxpayers still interested in sheltering what income they can, although they will be in the 45 or 50 percent tax brackets rather than 60 or 70 percent.

With the individual income tax cuts that will be phased in through 1983, even the numbers of people in those 45 or 50 percent tax brackets will shrink. In 1981, a married couple needed only $60,000 of taxable income to be in the 50 percent tax bracket; by 1984, they would need roughly $162,000. The likely result is a restructuring in the industry. Some shelters will be weeded out. Other new ones are likely to be set up, ones that will take best advantage of the new tax law and that appeal to taxpayers in the somewhat lower brackets.

"The economic elements of a project will become more important, and the tax benefits relatively less important," according to an analysis by Matthew J. Maryles and Arthur S. Ainsberg, who handle tax planning for the executives at Oppenheimer & Company. "To the extent that a tax shelter is a real investment, the new tax act will enhance its return. But to the extent that the attraction of the shelter was its high tax savings, the Act will reduce its attractiveness."

The new income tax ceiling, however, is only one of several blows that the new law deals to tax shelters. Beginning in 1982, the law also limits the tax credits that investors will be allowed to claim in certain shelters, such as art lithograph plates, book plates and records. In a lithograph tax shelter, for example, an investor might have put up $10,000 to buy a plate costing $100,000, promising to pay the remaining $90,000 out of profits from selling prints. Typically, the loan would later be forgiven. But the investor would already have taken an investment tax credit equal to the $10,000 invested. Under the new law, that won't be permitted.

In the only direct assault on a specific tax shelter, the new law also puts an end to deferring taxes through commodity trading. A trading technique known as the commodity straddle had been widely used to defer taxes, not only by commodity traders and Wall Street brokerage firms, but also by doctors, dentists, and other high-income individuals.

The Reagan administration mounted its offensive against tax shelters only partly to raise tax revenues. Closing the commodity trading loophole is expected to bring the Treasury an extra $1.4 billion in tax revenues each year. At the same time, cutting the top tax rate could work in the opposite direction, reducing revenues. What the White House hopes to accomplish by lowering the maximum tax rate is to channel money that would otherwise have flowed into tax shelters into more productive investments.

Not everyone is convinced this will happen. "We are already beginning to see people moving from one tax shelter to another, rather than avoiding tax shelters altogether," notes Thomas A. Russo, a partner at Cadwalader, Wickersham & Taft, a Wall Street law firm. "But tax shelters, both old and new, are being restructured to accommodate the new law."

While tax shelters will be hurt by some measures in the new tax law, they will benefit from others. Faster depreciation rates, in particular, could mean bigger tax deductions for many shelters. The lower capital gains tax will allow you to keep a greater percentage of the profits in tax shelters where there is a property, such as real estate, to be sold at a profit.

Even the reduction in the top income tax rate could be helpful to some investors in the 50 percent tax bracket. People in this bracket who invested in shelters under the old tax law sometimes found their tax shelter profits taxed at rates as high as 70 percent. In effect, then, they had converted income they had earned from working, which was taxed at a maximum rate of 50 percent, into income from investments, which could be taxed at rates as high as 70 percent. Under the new law, this could not happen, since there will no longer be any tax rate above 50 percent. The preferential tax treatment of some tax shelters also sometimes moved income taxed at 50 percent into a higher tax bracket under the old law. Under the new law, this can no longer happen.

The new law also increases the incentives for rehabilitating old buildings for business purposes. Many observers think the new incentives are so handsome that building rehabilitation could become a much more attractive tax shelter.

While the impact of the new law will vary from one shelter to the next, they will all be subject to the same new economics. Selling a tax shelter to someone in a tax bracket below 50 percent is not simply a matter of advertising. The economics of the tax shelter have to be good enough to warrant their interest. Previously, tax savings were of greater importance and financial success was seen by many investors as being secondary. Now, the economics of a project will have to carry more of the burden.

An Example: Subsidized Housing

By the time the new tax law had been signed, tax shelter sponsors had already begun to structure new offerings. Take the case of one tax shelter being marketed. Government-subsidized housing was a popular shelter even before the new tax law, because the Government gave it special breaks not available to other investments. But this shelter was clearly geared to the new tax era: All of its cash flow projections had been calculated for people at 45 or 50 percent tax rates.

For those unfamiliar with tax shelters, this project presents a fairly typical example. The total project cost of several million dollars was to be spread among many investors. Each investment unit cost $50,000, and the money would be collected over five years: $15,000 in the first year, $15,000 in the second, $9,000 in the third, $8,000 in the fourth, and $3,000 in the fifth.

For each dollar put up by the investors, the developer would borrow three more to help finance the project. In real estate shelters, investors are allowed to write off losses not only of the money they have invested, but also those represented by their share of the loans.

According to the projections for the project, each investor could claim $23,800 in losses the first year. To an investor in the 45 percent tax bracket, that tax deduction would be worth $10,700 in tax savings. (It would be worth even more to an investor in the 50 percent bracket.) Since the initial investment was only $15,000 in the first year, the investor would have recouped more than two-thirds of his investment in the first year. The losses in the next few years would also be very large.

There would be no cash flow from the project until the sixth year of the project, and even then, the income would be rather meager: about $1,000 annually for each investor. But by the seventh year, the large continuing losses, both from depreciation of the housing project and from operating losses, would generate enough tax deductions to pay back the investment.

By the end of 15 years, a typical lifetime for a subsidized housing project, the investor would have had losses of about $150,000, worth about $69,000 in tax savings, on a $50,000 investment. Combined with the investor's income of about $12,000 over the life of the project, the total return, before tax, would amount to about $81,000. (For an investor in the 50 percent tax bracket, the tax savings would have been even higher, and the total return before tax would be nearly $89,000.) At that time, chances are good that the housing project might not have any resale value. But if it could be sold, the price would represent further profits to investors, although they would then have to pay taxes on losses they had taken that exceeded their investment. Even then, however, they would have deferred these payments, and had the use of the money for many years.

Other Examples

Each tax shelter investment is subject to somewhat different rules, but the general pattern would be similar: The investor would look to substantial losses to provide tax savings, and that would represent much of the gain on the investment. On an industry-by-industry basis, the new tax law is expected to have the following effect on tax shelters:

OIL AND GAS: Investors in oil and gas shelters already benefit from special tax rules that allow the bulk of the drilling expenses — such as exploration costs — to be written off all at once, rather than over the life of the oil well. The faster depreciation rules will allow faster write-offs for the costs of the drilling rig and other tangible property and equipment. Under the new law, the reductions in the so-called windfall profits tax on oil are expected to enhance the attractiveness of oil and gas shelters only slightly.

But the new tax law does give oil and gas investors one other source of possible tax relief. The relief involves the amount that an investor's deductions exceed those he would have been able to claim without the special treatment for the immediate write-off of drilling costs. This excess amount is known as tax preference. The old law levied a special tax on these tax preferences, and that tax remains under the new law. But the preference items also pushed other income that was subject to a tax ceiling of 50 percent into higher tax brackets. And since there will no longer be a tax bracket greater than 50 percent, investors in oil and gas shelters will benefit from that change.

RENEWABLE ENERGY: These shelters (solar energy, windmills, underground steam, and so forth), have been exempted from the requirement that financing must come from third-party, arm's-length lenders for investors to be able to depreciate the capital value of the loans. To qualify for this exemption, such projects must now meet a test showing that they are making timely payments of their loans on a level-payment basis. Experts in renewable energy now think, however, that many of these shelters may not be able to meet this test.

REAL ESTATE: The new tax law permits buildings purchased any time after 1980 to be depreciated over 15 years. For investors who would have depreciated a building over a longer period, this new depreciation period will provide more tax deductions sooner. For aggressive investors who would have depreciated a building in 15 years or less under the old tax law, the new law will not provide any greater writeoffs, but it may save the trouble of a challenge from the Internal Revenue Service. The reduction in the top capital gains rate that has already taken effect should also mean greater profits to investors when they sell a building.

REHABILITATION OF OLD BUILDINGS: The new law provides more generous investment tax credits for the substantial rehabilitation of both historic and other buildings, provided they are to be used for business purposes. The nonhistoric buildings must also be nonresidential to qualify. A building that is between 30 and 39 years old is eligible for a credit equal to 15 percent of the rehabilitation costs. A nonhistoric building that is older brings a credit of 20 percent. Rehabilitating a certified historic structure earns a tax credit of 25 percent, but both the building and the rehabilitation plans need Government approval.

LITHOGRAGHS, BOOKPLATES, RECORDS: These shelters are still permitted. But the new rules prohibiting tax credits for financing that has not come from a third party could remove much of the attraction of such shelters.

COMMODITY TAX STRADDLES: The new law generally requires that profits and losses on all commodity futures contracts be recognized at year-end for tax purposes. This prevents an investor from taking offsetting long and short positions in the market, and cashing in on the losing position each year to show a tax loss, while postponing recognition of the gain until the following year.

RESEARCH AND DEVELOPMENT: The new tax law provides handsome tax credits for those companies engaged in ongoing research and development work. But newly formed tax shelters will probably not be able to take advantage of these credits. Furthermore, tax advisers predict that with the 25 percent credit, fewer companies will need investors to pay for their R. & D. costs.

LEASING: The new tax law also bars individual investors from cashing in on more generous leasing provisions. But leasing is expected to pick up as a corporate tax shelter, as corporations sell their credits and depreciation rights from leasing to other corporations.

While you are focusing on these more exotic shelters, you should not forget the simpler ones that are available: the new tax-exempt savings certificates and the expanded opportunities for tax-deferred retirement accounts. They may not be as much fun to discuss at a cocktail party, and you can not put as much money into them, but they do have the advantage that you can be certain of getting your money back.

Q: What is a tax shelter?
A: A tax shelter is an investment that helps you reduce or delay taxes. When people speak of tax shelters, typically they are referring to somewhat risky investments that may not show significant profits, but that provide a substantial portion of their return by giving you losses from the project as deductions on your tax return. Generally, tax shelters are structured as partnerships to allow you to take the losses as deductions, since you could not do this if your investment were in a corporation. Since deductions are worth the most to people in the highest tax brackets, most investors in tax shelters are in relatively high tax brackets.

Q: Should the average American family invest in tax shelters?
A: Many people are in tax shelters without really realizing it. If you have a mortgage on your house, for example, that is a kind of tax shelter, since you can take your interest payments as deductions from your income. If you invest in a tax-deferred retirement account or in the tax-exempt savings certificates, those are essentially. tax shelters too. As for other, more exotic tax shelters, you should be interested in them only if they show good evidence of providing

you with higher returns than other investments that are available. Since they are often more risky than other investments, you should be able to afford to lose the money you invest.

Q: How do I know whether a shelter is legitimate?

A: Try to make sure that the people running the tax shelter have a good track record on other projects. Make sure you read the prospectus for a project before investing. By learning as much as possible about the area you are investing in, you have a better chance of avoiding shelters that are less legitimate or have less chance of success. You might also seek the advice of your lawyer or accountant. Finally, if you have the money, you might consider investing in a diversified portfolio of shelters.

Q: While I was in the 70 percent tax bracket, I actively used tax shelters. Now that I am moving to the 50 percent tax bracket, should I still be interested in them?

A: Some shelters may still make good financial sense for you. But you should scrutinize them carefully. While you were in the 70 percent tax bracket, every dollar of loss in a project provided you with 70 cents of tax savings. In the 50 percent tax bracket, every dollar of loss provides you with only 50 cents of savings. Theoretically, you could look for larger losses — to generate more tax savings. But since the amount of your investment generally limits the losses you are allowed to write off, larger losses do not necessarily translate into larger tax deductions. Losses will still generate some tax savings for you under the new tax law. But you may want a project that generates more profits as well, to provide you with a suitable overall rate of return.

Q: I am in the 45 percent tax bracket. Now that tax shelters are being aimed at people in my tax bracket, should I invest in one?

A: Remember that if you were in the 45 percent tax bracket before the rate cuts began, you may be in a lower bracket by the time they finish. (If your income did not rise, you would move from a 45 percent to a 35 percent bracket.) So any calculations you make regarding the value of a tax shelter should take the lower tax rates into account.

Once you have ascertained what your future tax bracket is likely to be, you should focus on the potential for earnings that a tax shelter will offer. The decision to invest in a tax shelter should depend on what you will earn (and save on taxes) in the shelter, compared to what you can earn in other forms of investment. Some tax shelters may look good, others won't.

Q: My family is planning to buy a rundown building that has been certified historic and plan to live in it. Can we take the investment tax credit for rehabilitating historic structures?

A: You would be eligible for a 25 percent tax credit for the cost of substantially rehabilitating the building only if you rented it to someone else, or if you used it for other business purposes. Your rehabilitation plan must also be approved by the Secretary of the Interior. If you planned to live in it yourself, it would not qualify for the special tax credit.

Q: What buildings may be considered historic?

A: The building would be considered a historic structure if it is listed in the National Register or if it is located in a registered historic district and is certified by the Department of the Interior as being of historic significance to the district.

Q: How much money must be spent on a property for a rehabilitation to be considered "substantial" enough to qualify for the investment tax credit?

A: The rehabilitation expenses must be at least $5,000, and must generally exceed the value of the property, as determined by its "adjusted basis" for tax purposes.

14

Getting the Full Benefit

If you are put off by the potential for confusion among all the new tax provisions, you are not alone. Tax specialists who have grappled with the new law have run across many ambiguities, and are petitioning Congressional tax experts and the Treasury Department for clarifications. "There are lots of areas that are still vague, and lots of unanswered questions," notes Peter Elinsky, a partner with the accounting firm of Peat, Marwick, Mitchell. "The I.R.S. and the Treasury are going to have their hands full administering the new law properly."

Some of these matters will be cleared up through regulations. Others will be settled through litigation. But the information that is already available should be sufficient for most purposes; the important question is how to use it. There is no single agenda that will suit everyone, since not all of the provisions apply to everyone. Once you have an idea of what's in the law, you can figure out what applies to you. Remember, if you are single and in your first job, at a low salary, your options under the new law will be different from those of a prosperous middle-aged family, whose options will be different from those of a retired couple.

Take the case of a family with two children and income of about $70,000, split evenly between the husband and wife. That family could take advantage of the tax-deferred retirement accounts, the marriage penalty deduction, and the child care credits. According to calculations by Deloitte Haskins &

Sells, such a family under the old law might have paid $21,878 in taxes in 1980. In 1984, the same family with the same income, using the items mentioned above, together with the income tax rate cuts, might have reduced the family's taxes to $13,828.

If you have investment income and have been in a tax bracket higher than 50 percent, you can do even better, points out Ray J. Groves, chairman of Ernst & Whinney. He notes that under the individual income tax rate cuts, the maximum tax reduction for a single person without investment income is $4,707, and for a married couple without investment income, $8,278. On the other hand, since the new law will put a ceiling of 50 percent on the tax rate for investment income, there are much greater potential tax savings on investment income that had been taxed at rates as high as 70 percent.

This could make a real difference to people with high incomes. According to examples prepared by Ernst & Whinney, a couple with $250,000 in income in both 1980 and 1984 would realize a tax saving of only $8,278, if the whole income were from wages or other earned income. But if $50,000 of that income came from investments, the tax saving under the new law would amount to $17,970 by 1984.

If you are retired and no longer have earned income, you will not be eligible to use many of the new tax provisions, such as the marriage penalty deduction and the tax-deferred retirement accounts. But if you have investment income, the reductions in individual income tax rates will be of some help, and you might be interested in the tax-exempt savings certificates. If you sell your home and do not buy another one, you will be allowed to exclude from tax profits of $125,000 — rather than $100,000, provided you are 55 or older. The estate and gift tax rules could also be valuable.

Once you have figured out what applies to you, the next challenge will be keeping track of how the provisions change over the next few years. Often it seems as if the measures were constructed to confuse. The calendar at the end of this chapter should help you by outlining which provisions begin when, and how they change year by year. Confusing or not, there are bigger penalties now for getting things wrong.

One of the most striking examples of a provision that can't seem to sit still is the rule governing charitable contributions. Until now, people who did not itemize their tax deductions could not write off their contributions. Beginning in 1982, nonitemizers will be permitted to take tax deductions for contributions. But the change is effective for only five years, and the formula prescribing the permitted deduction changes four times during that period.

The first two years, nonitemizers will be allowed to deduct 25 percent of their contributions of up to $100. In 1984, the formula changes to 25 percent of contributions of up to $300. In 1985, the formula changes again, this time to 50 percent of all contributions. The following year, the lid is lifted entirely: Nonitemizers will be permitted to take tax deductions equal to 100 percent of their contributions. Then, in 1987, the situation returns to its former state: Nonitemizers will no longer be allowed to take any tax deductions for charitable contributions.

While this measure is one of the most skittish, many of the others also change annually. For example, the amount of income earned abroad that may be excluded from American taxes starts at $75,000 in 1982, and then rises by $5,000 a year until it reaches $95,000 in 1986. The amount that may be taken as a tax deduction to offset the "marriage penalty" if both spouses are employed rises between 1982 and 1983. The first year it equals 5 percent of the income — up to $30,000 — of the lower-earning spouse. In 1983 and after, it equals 10 percent of the income — up to $30,000 — of the lower-earning spouse.

Among the most potentially confusing of the phase-in rules are those covering estate and gift taxes, which involve several different phase-in periods. First, the new law gradually lowers the maximum tax to be paid on estates. That maximimum, now at 70 percent, will fall by 5 percentage points a year, to 65 percent in 1982, 60 percent in 1983, 55 percent in 1984, and 50 percent in 1985 and later years. At the same time, the lifetime allowance for tax-free gifts will be rising in somewhat erratic steps. That allowance, which now stands at $175,625, will rise to $225,000 in 1982, $275,000 in 1983, $325,000 in 1984, $400,000 in 1985, $500,000 in 1986, and $600,000 in 1987 and after.

Such changes could complicate estate planning. But tax experts say there are ways to write wills to take such changes into account. "You could set up your will to leave everything to your spouse except for the amount of lifetime credit you are entitled to, without specifying the amount," says Herbert Paul, of Touche Ross. "That would allow you to leave your heirs the most you could without its being taxed, and you would have phrased it so you don't need to rewrite your will each year."

But people whose wills already have such all-purpose phrases in them may still need to do some revising. The new tax law says that wills written before the new law was passed, and within 30 days after its passage, may still be interpreted as if the old law were in effect. For example, an old will calling for the spouse to receive whatever amount could be given tax-free would generally be interpreted to mean that the spouse would receive only half of the estate, despite the new law's provision that the whole estate may be given tax-free to one's spouse. The marital allowance under the old law permitted only half of the estate to be left to a spouse tax-free. Congress, however, was concerned that people may not have intended to leave their whole estate to their spouses, and therefore called for the old rules to apply to old wills, which did not specify amounts.

There are other transition rules that should also be taken into account. For example, people who sell their homes can exclude the profits from taxes if they buy a new house of at least equal value. Under the old law, the new home had to be purchased within 18 months before or after the sale of the old home to qualify for the special treatment; the new law extends the period to 24 months. While the new provision was aimed at home sales after July 20, 1981, it also includes any sales that occurred within 18 months prior to July 20.

Penalties for Mistakes

Taxpayers who take the care to sort through the new benefits of the new tax act should also acquaint themselves with some of the new penalties the law imposes.

WRONG INFORMATION: The penalties for providing wrong information on withholding forms after 1981 will rise sharply. The civil penalty will shoot to $500 from $50. The criminal penalty will rise to $1,000 from $500, although the potential prison sentence will remain limited to one year.

DELINQUENT PAYMENTS: The interest rate for delinquent payments will be set at the prime rate charged by commercial banks. A new rate will be set each October, based on the average bank rate during September. (This new interest rate will also apply to payments that the Government makes to taxpayers.) Previously, the rate was set at 90 percent of the prime rate and it was adjusted only every second year.

PROPERTY VALUATION: Overstating the value of a property on tax forms filed after 1981 will also be punished more severely. Penalties will be determined on a sliding scale based on the amount of overvaluation. Items overvalued by 50 to 100 percent will carry a penalty equal to 10 percent of the tax underpayment. Items overvalued by 101 to 150 percent will be charged 20 percent. And items that are overvalued by more than 150 percent will be penalized by an amount equal to 30 percent of the underpayment. Furthermore, if the overvaluation is deemed intentional or negligent, there will also be a second penalty equal to 50 percent of the interest payment already due on the underpayment of taxes. These penalties are expected to affect properties donated to charities as well as to tax shelter valuations.

Tax specialists say it is still too early to tell whether the new law will live up to the lofty aims of those who helped shape it: to lure people into working more and saving more, and to increase productivity and economic activity generally. The incentives being offered are huge. The reductions in individual income tax rates alone are expected to save taxpayers about $462 billion over five years, according to Congressional estimates, money that the Treasury would have been expected to collect had the law not been changed. Once the cost of other provisions aimed at individuals has been added in, the potential loss to the Treasury — and the savings to individuals — rises to about $572 billion.

Government economists hope to offset those revenue losses by holding down Government spending and through higher revenues from an economy bolstered by the tax cuts. But a lot depends on whether people understand the new law and make use of its various measures. Tax experts are urging clients to do just this.

"The best advice I can offer anyone," says Mr. Paul, of Touche Ross, "is that the new tax law has something in it for everyone, but you have really got to actively do things to take full advantage of the law."

Indeed, that is the clear message from nearly all tax experts who have pored over the 292 pages of provisions in the new tax law: This is an opportunity for you to save thousands of dollars in taxes over the next five years, but the burden is on you.

A CHECKLIST OF NEW PROVISIONS IN THE TAX LAW AND WHEN THEY TAKE EFFECT

1981

June 9

Investors who take long-term capital gains after this date will pay no more than 20 percent tax on those gains.

June 23

Commodity trading positions entered into after this date will be subject to the new tax provisions. Investors may also elect to apply the new rules to positions held on this date or earlier in the same tax year.

July 20

People who sell their homes after this date have 24 months, rather then 18 months, to buy a new house and avoid paying taxes on profits from the sale of the first home. The 24 month period will also apply to people who sold homes no more than 18 months before this date.

October 1

Individual income tax rates reduced 5 percent, in the first of three reductions.

October 1

The new tax-exempt "all-savers" certificates go on sale. They will be available only for 15 months, until Dec. 31, 1982.

1982

January 1

The maximum tax on unearned income falls to 50 percent from 70 percent.

Married couples with two earners may take a tax deduction equal to 5 percent of the income of the lower earner, up to $30,000. (Maximum deduction: $1,500.)

Anyone with earned income may set up a tax-deferred retirement account known as an individual retirement accounts, or I.R.A. He or she may contribute up to 100 percent of wages, up to a ceiling of $2,000. Anyone covered by other pension plans is now eligible for I.R.A.'s.

Expanded limits on contributions to Keogh plans, the tax-deferred retirement accounts specifically for the self-employed. The new contributions may go as high as $15,000 a year.

Americans working abroad may exclude up to $75,000 of foreign earned income from United States taxes.

Those who do not itemize deductions may take a tax deduction of 25 percent of their charitable contributions of up to $100. (Maximum deduction: $25.)

A new formula takes effect for calculating tax credits for workers who must pay for the care of children or other dependents.

The maximum estate tax is reduced to 65 percent from 70 percent.

Married people may give unlimited sums to their spouses through gifts or bequests, under a new unlimited marital deduction.

The ceiling on tax-free gifts rises. Each person may now give tax-free gifts of up to $10,000 per recipient to as many people as desired each year. The previous limit was $3,000.

The lifetome allowance on gifts or bequests that may be given tax-free to anyone (besides a spouse) rises to $225,000 from $175,625. This allowance does not include gifts that come within the annual giving limits.

Penalties rise for overvaluations of properties and for providing false information on withholding forms.

July 1

Individual income tax rates cut 10 percent, in the second tax cut.

December 31

The last day to buy tax-exempt saving certificates.

1983

January 1

The tax deduction available to married couples with two incomes rises to 10 percent of the income of the lower-earning spouse, up to a limit of $30,000 of income. (Maximum deduction: $3,000.)

Americans working abroad may exclude up to $80,000 of foreign earned income from United States taxes.

The lifetime tax-free gift allowance rises to $275,000.

The maximum tax on estates falls to 60 percent.

July 1

Income tax rates are cut 10 percent, in the third and final reduction.

1984

January 1

Americans working abroad may exclude up to $85,000 of foreign earned income from United States tax.

The deduction that those who do not itemize tax deductions may take for charitable contributions rises to 25 percent of contributions of up to $300. (Maximum deduction: $75.)

The lifetime tax-free gift allowance rises to $325,000.

The maximum tax on estates falls to 55 percent.

1985

January 1

Indexing of individual income tax rates begins.

Americans working abroad may exclude up to $90,000 of foreign earned income from United States tax.

Those who do not itemize deductions may deduct up to 50 percent of their charitable contributions.

The lifetime tax-free gift allowance rises to $400,000.

The maximum tax on estates falls to 50 percent for this year and future years.

1986

January 1

Americans working abroad may exclude up to $95,000 of foreign earned income from United States tax for this year and future years.

Those who do not itemize deductions may deduct 100 percent of their charitable contributions.

The lifetime tax-free gift allowance rises to $500,000.

1987

January 1

Those who do not itemize deductions may no longer deduct charitable contributions.

The lifetime tax-free gift allowance rises to $600,000 for this year and future years.

Index

ABOUT THE AUTHOR

Karen Wattel Arenson has worked as a financial reporter for *The New York Times* since 1978, covering Wall Street, financial markets, banking, and other business and economics topics. When the Reagan tax bill was being debated in Congress, *The Times* sent her to Washington to report on the progress of the tax package and on its implications. After the bill became law, she wrote a series of articles explaining the new law, and how individuals could make it work for them.

Born on Long Island, Karen Arenson graduated from the Massachusetts Institute of Technology, where she majored in economics. She also earned a master's degreee in public policy from the Kennedy School of Government at Harvard, and studied accounting and finance at the graduate school of management at Northwestern University. Prior to working at *The New York Times,* she worked for five years as a reporter and editor at *Business Week.*